Bahá'í Stories

My Journey to the Bahá'í Faith
Jeanie Halstead

While every precaution has been taken in the preparation of this book, the publisher assumes no responsibility for errors or omissions, or for damages resulting from the use of the information contained herein.

BAHA'I STORIES

First edition. November 12, 2022.

Copyright © 2022 Jeanie Halstead.

ISBN: 979-8215930014

Written by Jeanie Halstead.

Table of Contents

Dedication

The cover design is a nine-pointed crocheted star that my mother, Dorothy Mae Boggs-Womack made, as she knew how important the number nine was to me. I embellished it with symbols of the four kingdoms of God's creation. The colored stones represent the mineral kingdom, the morning glory leaves are the plant kingdom, the feathers the animal kingdom, and the pictures of various people the human kingdom. The Bahá'í writings say that the number nine is "the number of perfection" and "the highest digit, hence symbolizes comprehensiveness, culminations."

"Nine, as the highest single-digit number, symbolizes completeness. The Bahá'í Faith regards humanity as an organic entity which has developed through its embryonic state to infancy, then to adolescence and is now coming of age, which is the state of fulfilment; so likewise the number nine reflects a sense of fulfilment or culmination and perfection. Bahá'í Houses of Worship, for example, have nine sides, and one commonly used symbol of the Bahá'í Faith is a nine-pointed star. Nine is the minimum number of members in a Spiritual Assembly or House of Justice, the administrative bodies elected by Bahá'ís around the world."

Universal House of Justice, The Nine-Pointed Star: History and Symbolism, 24 January 1999

Author's acknowledgement: The author is in good standing and accepts the Universal House of Justice and its Institutions, however this book is an individual branch course initiative and not an official document of the Faith or its Institutions. The Bahá'í Faith has no clergy, is the planet's only Democratically elected Faith, and no individual or institution can interpret its Scriptures to another person.

MY JOURNEY TO THE BAHÁ'Í FAITH

For a long time in my early twenties, as a Christian, I was searching for answers, and going to different churches. At one church I asked them about the classes they were offering, and if they were teaching anything new. They said, "no it's pretty much the same things." I remember at one point I was sitting in my apartment and looking at the pretty tassels I had sewn on a curtain (odd how you remember extraneous things when you're contemplating important things), and asking myself, "Jesus, You said You were going to come back, so what is that going to be like, and when are You coming?" Nothing I was hearing, satisfied my mind and heart.

When my fiancé and I were looking for a place to get married we were riding on his motorcycle on a Sunday on Sheridan Rd and went past the Bahá'í House of Worship in Wilmette Illinois. I was awestruck, as he told me what it was. He didn't know much about the Faith, but he told me he knew some Bahá'ís and that they were very thoughtful people. Later, I phoned the House of Worship and arranged to go and talk to them.

I learned there was no charge for getting married there, and that it was a legally recognized service. They wouldn't take any money as a donation because only Bahá'ís can give to the fund. If a person is not a Bahá'í, and gives money, it is then given to a charity. So, when we did donate, it was given to a home for the elderly. I later learned about the honor and privilege of giving to the Fund as a Bahá'í. This way the money is cleansed of any outside influence. Reminds me of Jesus throwing out the money changers in the Temple.

While I was talking to the people at the House of Worship, I learned a little about the Faith and I loved it all! They gave me a prayer book and a sample of a Bahá'í couple's readings for their wedding. I used one of the prayers for our program which I created and had copied. It was pretty much a do-it-yourself-wedding! Also, there are no clergy in the Faith so no one pronounces you married, and the only thing you have to say for the service is spoken individually by both the bride and groom in the presence of at least two witnesses acceptable by the Local Spiritual Assembly, "We will, verily, all, abide by the Will of God."

Another thing we had to do which all Bahá'ís have to do is get written permission from our parents to get married. This is quite unusual for Westerners because we're used to doing as we please, but for Bahá'ís we get to choose who we marry (quite different from countries where there are arranged marriages). Then the parents in their wisdom may give their permission. This way it preserves the unity of the family and demonstrates a gratefulness in the hearts of children for those who have given them life.

My parents were okay, but it took some convincing of his parents. We had to explain that by giving permission it didn't mean they had anything to do with the Bahá'í Faith. We did finally get their permission. The lady who took care of my daughter while I worked offered to have our reception at her lovely home. She was a very religious Christian person, and she thought my program was beautiful. I was busy cooking, baking my cake, and freezing ahead of time. The wedding turned out beautifully, and shortly after we moved from the Chicago area to an apartment in Oshkosh Wisconsin.

Eventually, we bought a house on Hazel St right next to the park and Lake Winnebago. I began to look for a connection with the Bahá'ís and started going to informal gatherings in the homes of

Bahá'ís where someone would give a short talk on a particular subject. I loved that it was very interactive with discussion and questions. It took about a year of going to meetings, and reading "Bahá'u'lláh and the New Era," and I decided that Bahá'u'lláh was Who He said He was and declared my belief on October 2nd, 1972, becoming enrolled as a Bahá'i. Will be forever grateful for the Oshkosh Bahá'ís who were welcoming, warm, and nurturing. The late 60s and 70s were such a wonderful, magical time of social change and spiritual renewal!

But I never left Jesus behind or denied Him. Still love Jesus and feel that by accepting Bahá'u'lláh I am honoring Him and can now acknowledge all the former Manifestations of God. The Oneness of all the religions is one of the three Onenesses of the Faith. In addition to the Oneness of all the religions - God is one – there is only one God though He is called by different names in different lands. Thirdly mankind is one. They are also referred to as the unity of God, unity of religion, and unity of mankind. Bahá'u'lláh's key theme is world unity. The goal of developing a new world society is a paramount need at the present time. The pivotal teaching of the Bahá'í Faith is that all human beings are equally God's creation regardless of gender, race, nationality, or creed and should be respected and treated without prejudice.

I remember when I was told about the three onenesses when I was at the Bahá'í House of Worship for the first time so long ago, and I asked them "Isn't it confusing trying to follow all the laws of each religion at the same time?" They then explained to me that "no we honor the previous ones but turn to the latest one, Bahá'u'lláh for our guidance."

It's called progressive revelation and the Manifestations (Abraham, Moses, Buddha, Jesus, Mohammed, etc) didn't all come at once. If you line Them up on a timeline you can see, there's a pattern of about every thousand years give or take a few hundred. It is God's ancient covenant with us to never leave us alone. Like our teachers in school all were educated at the same university but only taught what the students were capable of understanding for their age. We wouldn't deny our former teachers, we would thank them for the foundation they gave us to build on our body of knowledge and draw closer to God. It is as Christ said: "I have yet many things to say unto you, but ye cannot bear them now. Howbeit when he, the Spirit of truth, is come, he will guide you into all truth: for he shall not speak of himself; but whatsoever he shall hear, that shall he speak: and he will shew you things to come. He shall glorify me: for he shall receive of mine, and shall shew it unto you." (John 16:13 KJV) Bahá'u'lláh glorifies Christ in over one hundred tablets.

Each religion brings two kinds of laws, spiritual and physical. The *spiritual laws* are always the same and never change. They have to do with the virtues and principles we live by such as: love, faith, hope, charity, mercy, kindness, glory, honor, trustworthiness, honesty, patience, meekness, etc... the list is long. The golden rule is in all religions. "He should not wish for others that which he doth not wish for himself, nor promise that which he doth not fulfil." (Bahá'u'lláh, Kitab-i-Iqan p.194) "Lay not on any soul a load which ye would not wish to be laid on you, and desire not for any one the things ye would not desire for yourselves." (Gleanings From the Writings of Bahá'u'lláh p.128) The only way we can know the Unknowable Essence of God is through the Messengers chosen by God Who are the perfect Mirrors of the virtues.

The *physical laws* pertain to our everyday life at this point in our evolution on this planet and are for our protection and safety. For example, in the time of Moses he forbade the eating of pork. At that time, they didn't understand about parasites, and they didn't have refrigeration and proper cooking. So, they had to accept on faith that it was bad for them. Today we have the means to be safer if we choose to eat pork, so we need an update on the physical laws. This is one way that religions look different from each other, but these physical laws have to do with the needs of the time and the place where they came.

Bahá'ís believe that Bahá'u'lláh is God's latest Manifestation of God and that His laws fit perfectly and fulfill the needs of our world today. It is like having the latest software for your computer to make it run more smoothly.

Here are some core beliefs that Bahá'u'lláh taught:

- The oneness of mankind
- Universal peace upheld by a world government
- Independent investigation of truth
- The common foundation of all religions
- The essential harmony of science and religion
- Equality of men and women
- Elimination of prejudice of all kinds
- Universal compulsory education
- A spiritual solution to economic problems
- A universal auxiliary language

How would this bring the whole world the peace, unity, and security it so badly needs? Bahá'u'lláh's mission is the spiritual unification of the entire planet! So how can these principles be implemented? How can we make this happen? I'm a pretty practical person so that is what I wanted to know!

Bahá'u'lláh has given us the mechanism or means by which to effectively bring about world peace and unify the planet. One of the chief means to accomplish this is the Administrative Order, which is brought by Bahá'u'lláh and is new in the spiritual evolution of humankind. There are no clergy in the Faith so in order to provide us with guidance and administer the affairs of the community we have this beautiful and amazing Administrative Order. "...It has two arms, the **elected** and the **appointed**. The supreme governing institution of the Bahá'í Faith is the Universal House of Justice, situated in Haifa, Israel. Some features set apart the Bahá'í administration from similar systems of human government: elected representatives should follow their conscience, rather than being responsible to the views of electors; political campaigning, nominations and parties are prohibited; and religious authority was passed down from its founder to the Universal House of Justice."

The Elected:

On the local level Bahá'ís gather annually to elect nine Bahá'ís by secret ballot for their Local Spiritual Assemblies in a prayerful attitude with love and respect.

"Bahá'í elections do not include any sort of constituency for members – all members are considered to be at-large. Members are chosen by the electorate based on Shoghi Effendi's stated criteria consisting of five qualities:

"Let us recall His explicit and often-repeated assurance that every Assembly elected in that **rarefied atmosphere of selflessness and detachment** is in truth, appointed of God, that its verdict is truly inspired, that one and all should submit to its decision unreservedly and with cheerfulness ... the elector ... is called upon to vote for none but those whom **prayer and reflection have inspired him** to uphold... Hence it is incumbent upon the chosen delegates to consider **without the least trace of passion and prejudice, and irrespective of any material consideration**, the names of only those who can best combine the **necessary qualities of unquestioned loyalty, of selfless devotion, of a well-trained mind, of recognized ability and mature experience**... Nothing short of the all-encompassing, all-pervading power of His Guidance and Love can enable this newly enfolded order to gather strength and flourish amid the storm and stress of a turbulent age, and in the fullness of time vindicate its high claim to be universally recognized as the one Haven of abiding felicity and peace."

The Universal House of Justice further clarified that the elector, having determined those who meet these qualifications, should give "due consideration. . . to such other factors as age distribution, diversity, and gender."

On the national level a nation is divided into local districts or units and Bahá'ís hold a local convention once a year to elect their one or more delegates by the same criteria as the members of the Local Spiritual Assembly were elected. These delegates will then go to the National Convention held once a year to elect the nine members of the National Spiritual Assembly.

Every five years members of the National Spiritual Assemblies are called to go to the International Convention at the Bahá'í World Center in Haifa Israel to vote for the nine members of the Universal House of Justice. The Universal House of Justice can both make new Bahá'í law and repeal its own laws, but It may not alter the scriptural laws defined by Bahá'u'lláh and 'Abdu'l-Bahá.

The Appointed:

"The appointed members act as individuals. While they have no authority to command or rule on matters, they are "the learned" and individuals and institutions are morally obliged to consider their opinions. These individuals inspire, encourage, enjoin, and make the community aware of relevant scripture and guidance from the central institutions. Their function is loosely defined, though their duties are divided into the two general categories of protection and propagation of the Bahá'í Faith. The learned have a similar geographic hierarchy. There are International Counselors, Continental Counselors, Auxiliary Boards, and their Assistants."

A key point of the process of administration is the practice of consultation. 'Abdu'l-Bahá states "The prime requisites for them that take counsel together are purity of motive, radiance of spirit, detachment from all else save God, attraction to His Divine Fragrances, humility and lowliness amongst His loved ones, patience and long-suffering in difficulties and servitude... The members thereof must take counsel together in such wise that no occasion for ill-feeling or discord may arise. This can be attained when every member expresseth with absolute freedom his own opinion and setteth forth his argument.

Should anyone oppose, he must on no account feel hurt for not until matters are fully discussed can the right way be revealed. The shining spark of truth cometh forth only after the clash of differing opinions. If after discussion, a decision be carried unanimously, well and good; but if the Lord forbid, differences of opinion should arise, a majority of voices must prevail."

Amanda Ripley, professional long form journalist since 2004 for *Time magazine*, 2009 for *The Atlantic*, and onward through other major news outlets, in her 2021 book *High Conflict: why we get trapped and how we get out*, describes the Bahá'í administration electoral and system of governance saying "...everything about these elections is designed to reduce the odds of high conflict." indeed that "The Bahá'ís try to select people who do not crave attention and power." and "In every meeting, they follow a protocol called 'consultation,' and it's designed to allow people to speak their mind without getting too attached to their own brilliance." In Ripley's summation "If social scientists designed a religion, it would look like this.... In this way, Bahá'í elections are ... designed to exploit the human capacity for cooperation, rather than competition."

Something that is the opposite of other world governments is that in Bahá'í administration the position seeks the person and not the other way around, as in "running for office." "One of the remarkable features of the Cause of God is that it does not harbour egotistical personalities. Its watchword is servitude, a servitude which is real and complete and which manifests itself in the form of humility and self-effacement." (The Revelation of Bahá'u'lláh, Vol. I p.133)

On a practical note, as we try to "walk the mystical path with practical feet", when all nine members of an assembly are present you can't have a tie vote, and you might actually get something done!

A good summary of the above is available under "Bahá'í Administration" on Wiki.

I hope I have been able to convey to you how and why I became a Bahá'í. The choice of one's religion is a deeply personal journey and is theirs alone to make. One of the principles listed above is the "Independent Investigation of Truth" which is necessary to validate one's beliefs and make them real instead of something that is parroted and just a comfortable custom. If a person were to decide they wanted to join the Bahá'í Faith, they would declare their belief in Bahá'u'lláh by signing a declaration card and attempt to follow the teachings. These twin duties are inseparable. Bahá'ís, just like all human beings are not perfect, but are sincere in their efforts to improve each day. Thanks be to a merciful God for do-overs! For me I try to be humble before God, be of service to others, seek guidance through the Writings, prayer, and meditation, and choose to be happy. The purpose of all the changes that come with each new Revelation is human happiness! It's really about the emotions of the Kingdom. That mystical connection to God! Religion must appeal to our reason and our hearts. One thing that will lead to understanding about this Faith is to read the history or the story about Bahá'u'lláh's life. And in fact, there are twin Manifestations in the Faith. The Báb (it means The Gate) came before Bahá'u'lláh (the Glory of God), and he prepared the way for Bahá'u'lláh much like John the Baptist for Christ. In Christianity, if you read the story of Jesus Christ's life you fall in love with Him. So too will you fall in love with Bahá'u'lláh and the Báb!

Wishing you Love, Peace, and Happiness,
Jeanie

HOW TO RECOGNIZE A PROPHET OF GOD

"The life of a Manifestation of God is fundamentally different from that of other human beings, and His greatness cannot be comprehended through a mere study of the events surrounding Him. During the years that He lives on earth, His extraordinary powers are diffused over the entire planet, causing a profound change in the reality of all created things, and preparing humanity for a new stage of progress. Though to external eyes His life may appear to be filled with afflictions, spiritual eyes discern in each event the signs of His glory and majesty." (Ruhi Book 4 p.1) God's Manifestations meet certain criteria that are the proof They are chosen by God. There are examples of these proofs for each Manifestation of God. Jesus Christ gave us the true template when He told us what to look for and to beware of false prophets. He said, "... by their fruits you will know them." – (Matthew 7:16. KJV) Since this is the story of The Báb and Bahá'u'lláh, here are some ways to know that They are Manifestations of God. Of course, however it is not an exhaustive list:

They all had innate knowledge.

The Báb: "The Báb belonged to a distinguished and noble family that traced its ancestry to Muhammad, the Prophet of Islam. His father passed away when He was a small child, and He was raised by His maternal uncle, who placed Him in school at an early age. Although the Báb was endowed with innate knowledge and did not need to be instructed by any man, He followed His uncle's wishes. His teacher, however, quickly recognized the Báb's great capacity and realized he had nothing to teach this extraordinary child." (The Dawn-Breakers pp. 75-76)

Bahá'u'lláh: "In His letter to Náṣiri'd-Dín S͟háh, the ruler of Persia, which refrains from any rebuke concerning His imprisonment in the Síyáh-C͟hál and the other injustices He had experienced at the king's hand, Bahá'u'lláh speaks of His own role in the Divine Plan: ("Bahá'u'lláh" – "Not of My Own Volition" The Baha'i International Community p. 25)

"This Wronged One hath frequented no school, neither hath He attended the controversies of the learned. By My life! Not of Mine own volition have I revealed Myself, but God, of His own choosing, hath manifested Me. In the Tablet, addressed to His Majesty the S͟háh—may God, blessed and glorified be He, assist him—these words have streamed from the tongue of this Wronged One: I was but a man like others, asleep upon My couch, when lo, the breezes of the All-Glorious were wafted over Me, and taught Me the knowledge of all that hath been. This thing is not from Me, but from One Who is Almighty and All-Knowing. And He bade Me lift up My voice between earth and heaven, and for this there befell Me what hath caused the tears of every man of understanding to flow. The learning current amongst men I studied not; their schools I entered not. Ask of the city wherein I dwelt, that thou mayest be well assured that I am not of them who speak falsely." (Epistle to the Son of the Wolf p. 11.)

They were all persecuted, denied, tortured and or martyred.

The Báb: He was martyred under most unusual and miraculous circumstances. You will learn about this in the story of The Life of The Báb.

Bahá'u'lláh: "Bahá'u'lláh was condemned, tortured and imprisoned. His possessions were taken from him, he was spat upon, ridiculed, stoned and poisoned. He was thrown into a pitch-black underground dungeon, icy cold, damp, and infested with vermin. A heavy chain was placed on his neck; his feet were put in stocks. He was exiled four times from Tehran in Persia to Baghdad in Iraq, to Constantinople and Adrianople in Turkey, to Akka in Palestine. He spent most of his life as a prisoner.

It's not that he did anything wrong. Rather, the Muslim clergy collaborated with the Persian and Turkish governments to do everything in their power to try to destroy what they felt was a dangerous, fast-growing heresy, and to suppress and destroy the progressive Baha'i teachings." (7 Proofs of Bahá'u'lláh's Mission – BahaiTeachings dot org Marty Schirn)

"Glory to Thee, O Thou Who art the Lord of all worlds, and the Beloved of all such as have recognized Thee! Thou seest me sitting under a sword hanging on a thread, and art well aware that in such a state I have not fallen short of my duty towards Thy Cause, nor failed to shed abroad Thy praise, and declare Thy virtues, and deliver all Thou hadst prescribed unto me in Thy Tablets. Though the sword be ready to fall on my head, I call Thy loved ones with such a calling that the hearts are carried away towards the horizon of Thy majesty and grandeur." - Bahá'u'lláh, Prayers and Meditations by Bahá'u'lláh, pp. 170-171

Their teachings revolutionized the spiritual lives of Their followers, and many followers shared in the persecution of the Manifestation.

The Báb's and Bahá'u'lláh's teachings so changed the lives of the believers that they were willing to sacrifice their lives for the Cause. Reading Their stories, you will learn about the torture and martyrdom of the early believers. "Since the beginning of the Cause, there have been at least ten thousand men who went with gladness to suffer martyrdom, and people who saw them suffering this martyrdom thought it was through their own power and did not know that a breeze had shaken them." 'Abdu'l-Bahá, Bahá'í Scriptures, p. 499

All the religions have a Holy Scripture that the followers try to adhere to.

The Báb brought the Bayan and Bahá'u'lláh gave us the Most Holy Book - The Book of Laws – The Kitáb-i-Aqdas

God sent all His Prophets into the world with one aim, to sow in the hearts of men love and goodwill, and for this great purpose they were willing to suffer and to die. All the sacred Books were written to lead and direct man into the ways of love and unity... (Abdu'l-Bahá, Paris Talks, p. 106)

They all made prophecies.

"Some have come true; some are coming true today. Here's one from the past. Bahá'u'lláh wrote letters to the rulers and ecclesiastical leaders of his time. Among them was Napoleon III.

Bahá'u'lláh condemned Napoleon's desire for military glory and the launching of the Crimean War. Here's an excerpt from his tablet to Napoleon III, revealed in 1868:

"For what thou hast done, thy kingdom shall be thrown into confusion, and thine empire shall pass from thine hands, as a punishment for that which thou hast wrought." – Bahá'u'lláh, The Proclamation of Bahá'u'lláh, p. 20.

Two years later, in the Battle of Sedan, Napoleon suffered the greatest defeat in military history up to that time. He was taken prisoner, his Empire collapsed and the French Republic was established." (7 Proofs of Bahá'u'lláh's Mission – BahaiTeachings dot org Marty Schirn)

In the area of science Bahá'u'lláh wrote: "Strange and astonishing things exist in the earth but they are hidden from the minds and the understanding of men. These things are capable of changing the whole atmosphere of the earth and their contamination would prove lethal." (Bahá'u'lláh, Kalímát-i-Firdawsíyyih (Words of Paradise), c.1879-91)

Some point to this as a statement about the discovery of nuclear energy and the use of nuclear weapons. Bahá'u'lláh also wrote that planets would be found around other star systems, and that life would be found on those planets: "Know thou that every fixed star hath its own planets, and every planet its own creatures, whose number no man can compute." (Gleanings from the Writing of Bahá'u'lláh, p.163)

They prophesied the time and conditions of the coming of the next Messenger of God.

"Bahá'u'lláh in the Kitáb-i-Aqdas stated that the next Manifestation of God will not appear before 1000 years have passed:

"Whoso layeth claim to a Revelation direct from God, ere the expiration of a full thousand years, such a man is assuredly a lying impostor. We pray God that He may graciously assist him to retract and repudiate such claim. Should he repent, God will, no doubt, forgive him... Whosoever, interpreteth this verse otherwise than its obvious meaning is deprived of the Spirit of God and of His mercy..."

(Bahá'u'lláh, Kitáb-i-Aqdas, 1873 p. 346)

They fulfilled prophecies:

"Bahá'u'lláh fulfilled countless prophecies contained in all the holy books. Here's one:

He who overcomes, I will make him a pillar in the temple of My God, and he shall go out no more. I will write on him the name of My God and the name of the city of My God, the New Jerusalem, which comes down out of heaven from My God. And *I will write on him My new name.*" – Revelation 3:12.

From this prophecy, it is evident that Christ will not return with the same name. He will be a different person, just as Christ was different from Moses. Baha'is believe that Bahá'u'lláh fulfilled these prophecies, and many others from diverse Faiths." (7 Proofs of Bahá'u'lláh's Mission – BahaiTeachings dot org Marty Schirn)

"For the Son of man shall come in the glory of his Father (Bahá'u'lláh means the Glory of God or the Father) with his angels; and then he shall reward every man according to his works." – Matthew 16:27.

How They lived Their lives and what history has written is a direct testament to and reflection of Their Teachings.

In reading Their stories, you will learn how They lived Their lives, and that it is indeed a testament to and a reflection of Their Teachings.

"Know thou of a certainty that the Unseen can in no wise incarnate His Essence and reveal it unto men. He is, and hath ever been, immensely exalted beyond all that can either be recounted or perceived. From His retreat of glory His voice is ever proclaiming: "Verily, I am God; there is none other God besides Me, the All-Knowing, the All-Wise. I have manifested Myself unto men, and have sent down Him Who is the Day Spring of the signs of My Revelation. Through Him I have caused all creation to testify that there is none other God except Him, the Incomparable, the All-Informed, the All-Wise." He Who is everlastingly hidden from the eyes of men can never be known except through His Manifestation, and His Manifestation can adduce no greater proof of the truth of His Mission than the proof of His own Person." Gleanings from the Writings of Bahá'u'lláh p. 49

They all established a religion that has stood the test of time.

There are approximately five million believers worldwide. The Baha'i Faith is established in virtually every country and in many dependent territories and overseas departments of countries. Baha'is reside in well over 100,000 localities. About 2100 indigenous tribes, races and ethnic groups are represented in the Baha'i community. ... Baha'i literature has been translated into more than 800 languages. – The Baha'i World News Service.

With these criteria in mind here is the story of the "Life of The Báb" and then the "Life of Bahá'u'lláh."

THE LIFE OF THE BÁB

Twenty-three May 1844 marked the beginning of a new era in human history. For centuries, all the peoples of the world have awaited the Promised Day of God, a Day when peace and harmony would be established on earth. The dawn of this new Day witnessed the appearance of not one but two Manifestations of God, the Báb and Bahá'u'lláh, Whose Revelations released the spiritual forces destined to transform society in accordance with the Will of God.

The Dispensation of the Báb began in 1844 and lasted only nine years. Its primary purpose was to prepare the way for the coming of Bahá'u'lláh. Although brief, the Báb's Dispensation was of such tremendous spiritual intensity that its effect will be felt for hundreds of generations to come.

The Báb, Whose name was Sayyid ʿAlí Muhammad , was born on 20 October 1819 in Shiraz, a city in southern Iran, also known as Persia. Most of the people in Iran belong to a Sect of Islam that awaits the coming of a Promised One of God called the Qa'im. The word "Qa'im" means He who ariseth.

The Báb belonged to a distinguished and noble family that traced its ancestry to Muhammad, the Prophet of Islam. His father passed away when He was a small child, and He was raised by His maternal uncle, who placed Him in school at an early age. Although the Báb was endowed with innate knowledge and did not need to be instructed by any man, He followed His uncle's wishes. His teacher, however, quickly recognized the Báb's great capacity and realized he had nothing to teach this extraordinary child. He has told the following story about the Báb's school days:

"One day," he related, "I asked the Báb to recite the opening words of the Qur'án: He hesitated, pleading that unless He were told what these words signified, He would in no wise attempt to pronounce them. I pretended not to know their meaning. 'I know what these words signify,' observed my pupil; 'by your leave, I will explain them.' He spoke with such knowledge and fluency that I was struck with amazement. He expounded the meaning of 'Alláh,' of 'Rahmán,' and 'Rahím,' in terms such as I had neither read nor heard. The sweetness of His utterance still lingers in my memory. I felt impelled to take Him back to His uncle and to deliver into his hands the Trust he had committed to my care. I determined to tell him how unworthy I felt to teach so remarkable a child. I found His uncle alone in his office. 'I have brought Him back to you,' I said, 'and commit Him to your vigilant protection. He is not to be treated as a mere child, for in Him I can already discern evidences of that mysterious power which the Revelation of the Qa'im alone can reveal. It is incumbent upon you to surround Him with your most loving care. Keep Him in your house, for He, verily, stands in no need of teachers such as I.' His uncle sternly rebuked the Báb. 'Have You forgotten my instructions?' he said. 'Have I not already admonished You to follow the example of Your fellow-pupils, to observe silence, and to listen attentively to every word spoken by Your teacher?' Having obtained His promise to abide faithfully by his instructions, he bade the Báb return to His school. The soul of that child could not, however, be restrained by the stern admonitions of His uncle. No discipline could repress the flow of His intuitive knowledge. Day after day He continued to manifest such remarkable evidences of superhuman wisdom as I am powerless to recount. At last His uncle was induced to take Him away from the school of Shaykh Abid, and to associate Him with himself in his own profession. There, too, He revealed signs of a power and greatness that few could approach and none could rival." [1]

He then began to work with His uncle as a merchant in Bushíhr, a city southwest of Shíráz

It was in this period of His life that the Báb married Khadíjih. The following story about them is taken from ("The Bittersweet Love Story of the Báb and His Wife" composed by Kathy Roman in bahaiteachings dot org)

The Báb and Khadíjih were playmates as children. Being second cousins twice removed, they were playmates until they reached the age where, by the Islamic custom in Persian society, they were no longer allowed to see each other. Then when the Báb reached the age of 23, his mother began to search for a wife for her son.

At the same time, Khadíjih, who was 20 years old, had a vivid dream:

One night I saw in the world of dreams, Fatima, the daughter of Mohammed, coming to our house and desiring one of us to marry her son. My sisters and I welcomed her with affection and courtesy. When she sat down, she looked us over keenly, then arose from her seat, came forward and kissed my forehead. – Munírih Khánum, *Episodes in the life of Munírih Khánum, Marriage of Khadíjih to the Báb*, pp. 32-33.

Khadíjih further related:

Next morning I arose and felt light and buoyant, but I was ashamed to relate my dream to anyone. The afternoon of that very day the mother of the Báb came to our house. With my sisters we went to welcome her, and, to my surprise just as I had seen in my dream, she left her seat, came smilingly toward me, kissed my forehead and embraced me. After some general conversation she left. My eldest sister whispered into my ears that she had come to ask my hand for her son. I answered, 'How fortunate I am.' Then I related my dream of the previous night saying that the realization of this dream had brought to my heart great happiness. – Ibid.

The Báb and Khadíjih soon married, the young couple very much in love. But shortly after their marriage Khadíjih had a frightening dream. A ferocious lion had appeared in her courtyard and she held her arms around its neck. The lion dragged her around the courtyard 2 ½ times. When Khadíjih awoke the next morning she recounted the terrifying dream to her husband. He explained to her the meaning of the dream – that their lives together would not last for more than 2 ½ years. Thus began a turn in their lives as the couple prepared themselves for the many adversities to come.

A year later Khadíjih, pregnant with their first child, became critically ill during childbirth, endangering her and their baby's lives. The mother of the Báb, frightened for both mother and child, appealed to her son to save them. The Báb then took a mirror and wrote a prayer on it. He asked his mother to hold the mirror in front of his wife, Khadijih. Soon afterwards, a baby boy, who they named Ahmad, was delivered. But shortly after his birth, the baby died.

The Báb's mother was very angry and upset with her son that he could not save both mother and baby, but the Báb explained that God did not destine for him to have children.

Then the Báb, who loved his wife so dearly, wrote these words of consolation to her:

O well-beloved! ...Thou shalt not be a woman, like other women, if thou obeyest God in the Cause of Truth, the greatest Truth ... Be patient in all that God hath ordained. Verily, thy son, Ahmad, is with Fátimih, the Sublime, in the sanctified Paradise. – H.M. Balyuzi, The Báb, p. 47.

Khadijih, spiritually mature and enlightened, observed that her beloved husband was also not like a man among other men. But she had no idea just how much until one unforgettable night. Sometime before the Báb declared his mission, Khadijih Bagum had an amazing encounter with her husband. Late one evening, the Báb left their bed and did not return for hours. Becoming worried, Khadijih began to search for him. As described in the book, "Twin Divine Trees:"

... she saw the upper chamber of the House immersed in light. What was the source of all this light, and where had the lamps come from, she asked herself. But this was not tangible light; it was divine light, and she did not see it with her outward eyes but with her inner sight. ... There she saw that world-illuminating Sun and light-shedding Moon standing in the middle of the room with His hands raised heavenward. While her eyes were fixed upon the dazzling light emanating from His being, a feeling of awe and fright came over her. She wanted to return but was unable to move. Her awe grew to such intensity that she felt stupefied. – quoted by Baharieh Rouhani Ma'ani, *Twin Divine Trees*, p. 34.

The Báb would later say to her the next morning:

Know thou that the Almighty God is manifested in Me. I am the One whose advent the people of Islam have expected for over a thousand years. God has created Me for a great Cause, and you witnessed the divine revelation. Although I had not wished that you see Me in that state, yet God had so willed that there may not be any place in your heart for doubt and hesitation. – Ibid., p. 35.

Khadijih Bagum related that as soon as she heard The Báb speak these words, she believed in him ... and her heart became calm and assured. Later, the Báb revealed a special prayer for his beloved Khadijih to say in times when he was away or she was afraid for his safety. He said:

In the hour of your perplexity, recite this prayer ere you go to sleep. I Myself will appear to you and will banish your anxiety. – Nabil, *The Dawn Breakers*, p. 143.

The Báb and his wife Khadijih shared a life of intense sacrifice at a time that would later be known as "The Hour of the Dawn" – the beginning of a new world Faith. Despite fierce religious persecution, forced separation, and the tragic loss of their newborn son, the two remained steadfastly devoted to each other, and to God. The Báb described the sorrow he would feel when the couple was separated:

My sweet love ... God is my witness that since the time of separation sorrow has been so intense that it cannot be described ... – H.M. Balyuzi, *Khadijih Bagum: Wife of The Báb.*

The two newlyweds, very much in love, had so little time together on this Earth. But in that short time they cherished each day and triumphed over every adversity. Their love will endure until the end of time and they will be united throughout all the worlds of God.

As the Báb predicted, 2 ½ years after Khadijih's dream about the lion, he was martyred ... but that is yet another bittersweet love story." ("The Bittersweet Love Story of the Báb and His Wife" composed by Kathy Roman in bahaiteachings dot org)

During His youth, the Báb showed signs of a power and greatness that no one could rival. The extraordinary qualities that would distinguish Him throughout His swift and tragic Ministry were already manifest. The Guardian refers to Him as "the gentle, the youthful and irresistible person of the Báb, matchless in His meekness, imperturbable in His serenity, magnetic in His utterance" [2]. The sections that follow can but inadequately describe the events of His life. Yet even this brief account should ignite in our hearts a spark from the fire of love that He enkindled in the hearts of thousands and thousands of His followers.

Before the Báb declared His Mission, several people around the world knew deep in their hearts that the Promised One would soon appear. One of these saintly personages was Siyyid Káẓim, who lived in the city of Karbila in 'Iraq. Siyyid Káẓim had many students, and he devoted his life to preparing them for the long-awaited coming of the Qa'im. He repeatedly told them that after his death they should leave their homes and, with hearts free of all earthly desires, spread out in search of the Promised Beloved.

After the passing of Siyyid Káẓim, a most distinguished student of his, Mulla Husayn, went to a mosque and spent forty days in prayer and meditation, during which he opened wide his heart to God's inspiration. Having completed these forty days, he left 'Iraq with two companions and set out in search of the Promised One. He went first to Bushihr. But he did not remain there long, for something seemed to pull him irresistibly northwards, and he soon departed for Shiraz. Arriving at the gate of that city, he Instructed his two companions to go directly to the mosque and remain there until his arrival.

A few hours before sunset on that very day, while walking outside the gate of the city, he met a youthful Personage Who welcomed him and invited him to His home to refresh himself after his long and difficult journey. Mulla Husayn was deeply impressed by the gentle yet compelling manner in which this extraordinary Youth spoke. He followed Him, and soon they arrived at the gate of a modest house. They entered the house and were seated in the upper room. The gracious Host ordered a water-jug to be brought so that His guest could wash away the dust from his journey. Then, He Himself prepared tea and offered it to Mulla Husayn. After these acts of hospitality, He began to speak with His guest. The details of that historic conversation were later told by Mulla Husayn:

"It was about an hour after sunset when my youthful Host began to converse with me. 'Whom, after Siyyid Káẓim,' He asked me, 'do you regard as his successor and your leader?' 'At the hour of his death,' I replied, 'our departed teacher insistently exhorted us to forsake our homes, to scatter far and wide, in quest of the Promised Beloved. I have, accordingly, journeyed to Persia, have arisen to accomplish his will, and am still engaged in my quest.' 'Has your teacher,' He further inquired, 'given you any detailed indications as to the distinguishing features of the Promised One?' Yes, "I replied, 'He is of a pure lineage, is of illustrious descent, and of the seed of Fátimih. As to His age, He is more than twenty and less than thirty. He is endowed with innate knowledge. He is of medium height, abstains from smoking, and is free from bodily deficiency.' He paused for a while and then with vibrant voice declared: 'Behold, all these signs are manifest in Me!' He then considered each of the above-mentioned signs separately, and conclusively demonstrated that each and all were applicable to His person."[3]

During that night, the Báb demonstrated to Mulla Husayn, with clear and unmistakable proofs, that He was the Promised Qa'im. He revealed, with extraordinary rapidity, the first part of His commentary on the Surih of Joseph, an important chapter of the Qur'an. He then addressed Mulla Husayn in these words:

"O thou who art the first to believe in Me! Verily I say, I am the Báb, the Gate of God, and thou art the Bábu'l-Báb, the gate of that Gate. Eighteen souls must, in the beginning, spontaneously and of their own accord, accept Me and recognize the truth of My Revelation. Unwarned and uninvited, each of these must seek independently to find Me. And when their number is complete, one of them must needs be chosen to accompany Me on My pilgrimage to Mecca and Medina. There I shall deliver the Message of God to the Sharif of Mecca. I then shall return to Kufih, where again, in the mosque of that holy city, I shall manifest His Cause. It is incumbent upon you not to divulge, either to your companions or to any other soul, that which you have seen and heard."[4]

This glorious Revelation filled Mulla Husayn's soul with excitement and joy, with awe and wonder. "How feeble and impotent, how dejected and timid, I had felt previously!" he later said. "Then I could neither write nor walk, so tremulous were my hands and feet. Now, however, the knowledge of His Revelation had galvanized my being. I felt possessed of such courage and power that were the world, all its peoples and its potentates, to rise against me, I would, alone and undaunted, withstand their onslaught. The universe seemed but a handful of dust in my grasp. I seemed to be the Voice of Gabriel personified, calling unto all mankind: 'Awake, for, lo! the morning Light has broken. Arise for His Cause is made manifest. The portal of His grace is open wide; enter therein, 0 peoples of the world! For He Who is your Promised One is come!' " [5]

The Declaration of the Báb took place on the eve of 23 May 1844. He was twenty five years old. Many years later on the occasion of the anniversary of the Báb's Declaration, 'Abdu'I-Baha addressed a group of believers in the following words:

"This is 23 May, the anniversary of the message and Declaration of the Báb. It is a blessed day and the dawn of manifestation, for the appearance of the Báb was the early light of the true morn, whereas the manifestation of the Blessed Beauty, Bahá'u'lláh, was the shining forth of the sun. Therefore, it is a blessed day, the inception of the heavenly bounty, the beginning of the divine effulgence. On this day in 1844 the Báb was sent forth heralding and proclaiming the Kingdom of God, announcing the glad tidings of the coming of Bahá'u'lláh and withstanding the opposition of the whole Persian nation." [6]

After Mulla Husayn, seventeen other individuals sought and independently found their Heart's Desire, the Báb. Each was guided by God to recognize the truth of the newborn Revelation, some through visions or dreams, some through prayer, and others during moments of meditation. All but one of these blessed souls attained the Báb's presence in Shiraz. The one who did not meet Him. was a unique and talented woman called Tahirih. She came to know of the Báb through a dream, recognized Him as the Promised Beloved and became a great promoter of His Cause. The eighteenth person to join the ranks of His followers was a twenty-two-year-old youth known as Quddus. Although young, Quddus possessed an exemplary character, and courage and faith that few could equal. These first believers, together with Mulla Husayn, were declared by the Bib as the eighteen "Letters of the Living". They were His chosen apostles.

Soon after the number of the Letters of the Living was complete, the Báb called Mulla Husayn to His presence and gave him the following instructions:

"The days of our companionship are approaching their end. My Covenant with you is now accomplished. Gird up the loins of endeavor and arise to diffuse My Cause. Be not dismayed at the sight of the degeneracy and perversity of this generation, for the Lord of the Covenant shall assuredly assist you. Verily, He shall surround you with His loving protection, and shall lead you from victory to victory. Even as the cloud that rains its bounty upon the earth, traverse the land from end to end, and shower upon its people the blessings which the Almighty, in His mercy, has deigned to confer upon you...... In this pilgrimage upon which We are soon to embark, We have chosen Quddús as Our companion. We have left you behind to face the onslaught of a fierce and relentless enemy. Rest assured, however, that a bounty unspeakably glorious shall be conferred upon you. Follow the course of your journey towards the north, and visit on your way Isfahán, Ká<u>sh</u>án, Qum, and Tihrán. Beseech almighty Providence that He may graciously enable you to attain, in that capital, the seat of true sovereignty, and to enter the mansion of the Beloved. A secret lies hidden in that city. When made manifest, it shall turn the earth into paradise. My hope is that you may partake of its grace and recognize its splendor." [7]

Having given Mulla Husayn instructions to go to Tihran, the Báb summoned the other Letters of the Living to His presence and assigned to each one a special mission. In His parting words to them, He called upon them to lay aside every earthly desire and scatter far and wide to proclaim His Cause. "O My beloved friends!" He addressed them. "You are the bearers of the name of God in this Day... It behooves each one of you to manifest the attributes of God, and to exemplify by your deeds and words the signs of His righteousness, His power and glory." "Heed not your weaknesses and frailty," He assured them. "Fix your gaze upon the invincible power of the Lord, your God, the Almighty... Arise in His name put your trust wholly in Him, and be assured of ultimate victory." [8]

In October 1844 the Báb, accompanied by Quddus, set out on His pilgrimage to Mecca and Medina. These two cities, located in Arabia, are sacred for the followers of Islam. While in Mecca, the Báb wrote a letter to the Sharif of the city. In that letter, He clearly explained His Mission and called upon the Sharif to accept His Cause. But the Sharif, who was busy with bis own affairs, failed to respond to the Divine Messenger. From Mecca, the Báb went with His companion to Medina,. where the mortal remains of the Prophet Muhammad are enshrined. After visiting that holy city, they made their way back to Persia. Arriving in Bushihr, the Báb summoned Quddus to His presence and with these words instructed him to proceed to Shiraz:

"The days of your companionship with Me," He told him, "are drawing to a close. The hour of separation has struck, a separation which no reunion will follow except in the Kingdom of God.... In the streets of <u>Sh</u>íráz, indignities will be heaped upon you, and the severest injuries will afflict your body. You will survive the ignominious behaviour of your foes, and will attain the presence of Him who is the one object of our adoration and love. In His presence you will forget all the harm and disgrace that shall have befallen you. The hosts of the Unseen will hasten forth to assist you, and will proclaim to all the world your heroism and glory. Yours will be the ineffable joy of quaffing the cup of martyrdom for His sake. I, too, shall tread the path of sacrifice, and will join you in the realm of eternity." [9]

In Shiraz, Quddus began teaching the new Message with great fervor. But soon he faced opposition from the Islamic clergy and the governor of the province. The governor, a cruel and wicked man, ordered the arrest of Quddus and one of his companions. He commanded that their beards should be burned, that their noses be pierced with a hole through which a cord be passed, and that with this cord they should be led through the streets for all to see. "It will be an object lesson to the people of Shiraz," was the decree of the governor, "who will know what the penalty of heresy will be." [10] After suffering these indignities, Quddus and his companion were expelled from the city, being warned they would be put to death if they attempted to return. By their suffering, these two heroic souls earned the honor of having been the first to be persecuted in Persia for the sake of their new Faith. 'Abdu'l-Baha has referred to the thousands who were later persecuted in the path of their Beloved, the Báb, in these words:

"…. they suffered the most grievous difficulties and severe ordeals. They withstood the tests with wonderful power and sublime heroism. Thousands were cast into prison, punished, persecuted, and martyred. Their homes were pillaged and destroyed, their possessions confiscated. They sacrificed their lives most willingly and remained unshaken in their faith to the very end. Those wonderful souls are the lamps of God, the stars of sanctity shining gloriously from the eternal horizon of the will of God." [11]

Having ordered so unjust a punishment to be given to Quddus and his companion, the governor turned his anger towards the Báb. He sent his guards on horseback to Bushihr with instructions to arrest Him and to bring Him in chains to Shiraz. In the meantime, the Báb had left Bushihr for Shiraz. It was in the wilderness between these two cities that the mounted escort met Him. Much later, the leader of the escort told the story of that encounter:

"As we approached him, he saluted us and enquired as to our destination. I thought it best to conceal from him the truth and replied that in this vicinity we had been commanded by the governor of Fárs to conduct a certain enquiry. He smilingly observed: 'The governor has sent you to arrest Me. Here am I; do with Me as you please. By coming out to meet you, I have curtailed the length of your march, and have made it easier for you to find Me.' I was startled by his remarks and marvelled at his candour and straightforwardness. I could not explain, however, his readiness to subject himself, of his own accord, to the severe discipline of government officials, and to risk thereby his own life and safety. I tried to ignore him, and was preparing to leave, when he approached me and said: 'I swear by the righteousness of Him who created man, distinguished him from among the rest of His creatures, and caused his heart to be made the seat of His sovereignty and knowledge, that all My life I have uttered no word but the truth, and had no other desire except the welfare and advancement of My fellow-men. I have disdained My own ease and have avoided being the cause of pain or sorrow to anyone. I know that you are seeking Me. I prefer to deliver Myself into your hands, rather than subject you and your companions to unnecessary annoyance for My sake.' These words moved me profoundly. I instinctively dismounted from my horse, and, kissing his stirrups, addressed him in these words: 'O light of the eyes of the Prophet of God! I adjure you, by Him who has created you and endowed you with such loftiness and power, to grant my request and to answer my prayer. I beseech you to escape from this place and to flee from before the face of Husayn <u>Kh</u>án, the ruthless and despicable governor of this province. I dread his machinations against you; I rebel at the idea of being made the instrument of his malignant designs against so innocent and noble a descendant of the Prophet of God. My companions are all honourable men. Their word is their bond. They will pledge themselves not to betray your flight. I pray you, betake yourself to the city of Ma<u>shh</u>ad in <u>Kh</u>urásán, and avoid falling a victim to the brutality of this remorseless wolf.' To my earnest entreaty he gave this answer: 'May the Lord your God requite you for your magnanimity and noble intention. No one knows the mystery of My Cause; no one can fathom its secrets. Never will I turn My face away from the decree of God. He alone is My sure Stronghold, My Stay and My Refuge. Until My last hour is at hand, none dare assail Me, none can frustrate the plan of the Almighty. And when My hour is come, how great will be My joy to quaff the cup of martyrdom in His name!

Here am I; deliver Me into the hands of your master. Be not afraid, for no one will blame you.' I bowed my consent and carried out his desire." 12

The Báb immediately continued His journey to Shiraz. Free and without chains, He went before His guards, who followed Him respectfully. By the magic of His words, He had disarmed their hostility and had changed their pride and arrogance into humility and love.

Arriving in Shiraz, the Báb was brought before the governor, who treated Him with shameful cruelty, He publicly rebuked and criticized the Báb, He then released Him into the custody of His uncle. Although the Báb was allowed to return to His home, His freedom was restricted. Only the members of His family and a few others were permitted to see Him. Yet, over the months that followed, in spite of attempts by the governor and the clergy to put an end to His influence, the number of His followers rapidly increased.

The fame of the Báb soon became so great that the King sent one of his most trusted and knowledgeable scholars to Shiraz in order to investigate the situation. A guest in the home of the governor himself, the scholar, who would later be known as Vahid, met with the Báb on three occasions. Determined each time to refute the arguments of the Báb, he grew increasingly awed by His knowledge, eloquence, and wisdom. In the third meeting Vahid became utterly convinced of the Youth's Station. Later, referring to his meetings with the Báb, Vahid explained that he felt as "lowly as the dust beneath His feet". Vahid immediately sent a written report to the Kings court and left Shiraz at the instruction of the Báb. From that day forward, he dedicated is energies to the promotion of His Cause and eventually laid down his life in the path of his Beloved.

With the Báb's rising power and fame, the governor's anger grew and he again ordered His arrest. This time the governor intended to put the Báb to death. But, on the very night of His arrest, a plague broke out in Shiraz and the entire city was thrown into a state of panic.

Within a few hours, over a hundred people had died from the dreaded disease. A police official, whose son was miraculously cured by the Báb, recognized the Hand of God in the outbreak of this plague and pleaded with the governor to release the Báb. The governor, fearing for the lives of his family and the inhabitants of the city, accepted on condition that the Báb would leave Shiraz.

In the fall of 1846, the Báb departed for Isfahan, a city north of Shiraz. As He said farewell to His uncle, He told him: "I will again meet you amid the mountains of Adhirbayjan, from whence I will send you forth to obtain the crown of martyrdom. I Myself will follow you, together with one of My loyal disciples, and will join you in the realm of eternity." [13]

As the Báb neared the city of Isfahan, He wrote a letter to the governor of that province requesting him to appoint the place where He should live. Unlike the governor in Shiraz, this governor was a pure-hearted and just man. He was so moved by the courtesy and style of the Báb's letter that he instructed the highest religious official of the province to receive the Báb in his home and to give Him a warm and generous reception.

During the Báb's stay in Isfahan, His fame gradually spread throughout the entire city. Crowds of people came to see Him every day and listen to His words of wisdom. But the Báb's growing popularity aroused the jealousy of the clergy of the city, who were afraid of losing their own position and power. They began to spread rumors about the Báb, hoping to excite suspicion against Him. When this failed, they devised a plan to do away with Him. The governor, aware of the clergy's schemes against the Báb, decided it would be best to have Him come and stay in his own home. There, during hours spent in conversation with the Báb, the governor gradually came to understand the greatness of His Revelation. One day, while seated with the Báb in the garden of his home, the governor addressed Him in these words:

"The almighty Giver has endowed me with great riches. I know not how best to use them. Now that I have, by the aid of God, been led to recognize this Revelation, it is my ardent desire to consecrate all my possessions to the furtherance of its interests and the spread of its fame. It is my intention to proceed, by Your leave, to Tihrán, and to do my best to win to this Cause Muhammad <u>Sh</u>áh, whose confidence in me is firm and unshaken." [14]

To this outpouring of love and devotion, the Báb replied: "May God requite you for your noble intentions. So lofty a purpose is to Me even more precious than the act itself. Your days and Mine are numbered, however; they are too short to enable Me to witness, and allow you to achieve, the realization of your hopes. Not by the means which you fondly imagine will an almighty Providence accomplish the triumph of His Faith. Through the poor and lowly of this land, by the blood which these shall have shed in His path, will the omnipotent Sovereign ensure the preservation and consolidate the foundation of His Cause. That same God will, in the world to come, place upon your head the crown of immortal glory, and will shower upon you His inestimable blessings. Of the span of your earthly life there remain only three months and nine days, after which you shall, with faith and certitude, hasten to your eternal abode." [15]

Three months and nine days later the governor passed away, exactly as the Báb had foretold. A few days after his death, his successor sent a message to the King in Tihran asking him what he should do with the Báb. The King ordered him to send the Báb in disguise to the capital, where the King intended to meet Him. Thus, in the company of a mounted escort, the Báb began His journey to Tihran.

The Prime Minister of Persia at that time was a selfish and incompetent man. He was afraid that, if the Báb came to Tihrán and met the King, he would lose his own position and power. Therefore, he convinced the King to change his orders and send the Báb to the province of Adhirbayjan in the northwest of the country.

When the Báb arrived at Tabriz, the capital of the province, He was taken to one of the main houses of the city, where He was to be confined. A detachment of soldiers guarded the entrance of the house. No one was permitted to see Him except two of His followers. The people of the city were warned that whoever tried to meet the Báb would be thrown into prison and all his possessions would be taken away.

The Báb stayed in Tabriz for a short time and was then transferred to the fortress of Mah-Ku, situated in the mountains of Adhirbayjan far away from large cities and towns. The people of this region belong to a different sect of Islam, one which has many disagreements with the sect that the majority of the population follows. The Prime Minister had thought that by sending the Báb to this remote and inhospitable corner of the country, His influence would diminish, and His Faith would gradually be forgotten. But he did not realize that the lamp of the Religion of God had been lit and that no human hand could put out its flame. The Báb, through His majesty and loving-kindness, soon won the respect and admiration of both the official in charge of the fortress and the people of the region.

The severe discipline placed upon the Báb was gradually relaxed, and the doors of the fortress were opened to His followers, who came in increasing numbers from different parts of Persia to visit Him. During the period of His imprisonment in Mah-Ku, the Báb revealed the Persian Bayan, the most important of all His Works. In that Book, He established the laws of His Dispensation, plainly and directly announced the coming of another Revelation greater than His own, and urged His followers to seek and find "Him whom God would make manifest". One of His followers who lived in Mah-Ku at that time described the revelation of the Persian Bayan in these words:

"The voice of the Báb, as He dictated the teachings and principles of His Faith, could be clearly heard by those who were dwelling at the foot of the mountain. The melody of His chanting, the rhythmic flow of the verses which streamed from His lips caught our ears and penetrated into our very souls. Mountain and valley re-echoed the majesty of His voice. Our hearts vibrated in their depths to the appeal of His utterance." [16]

When the Prime Minister learned that the Báb had won the admiration of the people of Mah-Ku and that His Faith was continuing to spread throughout the country, he issued an order for the Báb to be transferred to the fortress of Chihriq. But, there too, the people of the surrounding towns and the official of the fortress were attracted to the magnetic personality of the Báb. Even some of the most distinguished clergy of the region accepted the new Faith and left their privileged positions to join His followers.

As soon as the Prime Minister heard of the Báb's growing popularity in Chihriq, he gave orders to have Him sent immediately to Tabriz. There, the government called a meeting of the religious authorities to examine the Báb and find the most effective way to put an end to His influence. At that meeting, the clergy and government officials tried to humiliate the Báb, but were overpowered by His majesty and greatness. When asked, "Whom do you claim to be, and what is the message which you have brought?" He declared:

"I am, I am, I am, the promised One! I am the One whose name you have for a thousand years invoked, at whose mention you have risen, whose advent you have longed to witness, and the hour of whose Revelation you have prayed God to hasten. Verily I say, it is incumbent upon the peoples of both the East and the West to obey My word and to pledge allegiance to My person." [17]

A few days after that meeting, the Báb was taken back to Chihriq. His enemies had hoped that by bringing Him to Tabriz they would force Him to give up His Mission. But in the end they were convinced that, as long as the Báb remained alive, it would be impossible to stop His growing influence.

In the year 1850, a new Prime Minister of Persia, as bloodthirsty as the previous one ordered the execution of the Báb. Again, the Báb was brought from Chihriq to Tabriz. There He was confined to a cell next to a courtyard, which was to be the scene of His martyrdom.

As the Báb was being conducted to the cell, a youth forced his way through the crowd and threw himself at the feet of the Báb. "Send me not from Thee, O Master," pleaded the youth. He begged the Báb to allow him to follow Him wherever He might go. "Arise," answered the Báb, "and rest assured that you will be with Me. Tomorrow you shall witness what God has decreed." [18] The youth was immediately arrested, together with two of his companions, and was placed in the same cell in which the Báb and His secretary were confined. This young man became known as Anis.

Anis had heard of the new Message from the Báb Himself when He was in Tabriz and had determined to follow Him to Chihriq. So strong was the fire of the love of God burning in Anis' heart that his only desire was to sacrifice himself for his new Faith. But his stepfather, alarmed at his son's strange behavior, confined Anis to his home and kept him under strict watch. There Anis spent weeks in prayer and meditation, imploring God to allow him to attain the presence of his Beloved. Then one day, while lost in prayer, he had an extraordinary vision. He saw the Báb standing before him and calling to him. Anis threw himself at His feet. "Rejoice," the Báb said to him, "the hour is approaching when, in this very city, I shall be suspended before the eyes of the multitude and shall fall a victim to the fire of the enemy. I shall choose no one except you to share with Me the cup of martyrdom. Rest assured that this promise which I give you will be fulfilled." [19] And so Anis began to wait patiently, knowing that the day would soon arrive when he would be reunited with his Beloved. Now, at last, he had attained his Heart's Desire.

That evening the Báb was aglow with joy. He spoke with cheerfulness to Anis and the other three loyal followers confined with Him in His prison cell. "Tomorrow", He said to them, "will be the day of My martyrdom. Would that one of you might now arise and, with his own hands, end My life. I prefer to be slain by the hand of a friend rather than by that of the enemy." None of them could think of taking so precious a life, and they remained silent, tears running from their eyes. Then, suddenly, Anis sprang to his feet and said he was ready to obey whatever the Báb might command. "This same youth who has risen to comply with My wish ," the Báb declared, "will together with Me, suffer martyrdom. Him will I choose to share with Me its crown." [20]

Early the next morning, 9 July 1850, the Báb was working with His secretary when an official suddenly interrupted their conversation. "Not until I have said to him all those things that I wish to say," the Báb told the official, "can any earthly power silence Me. Though all the world be armed against Me, yet shall they be powerless to deter Me from fulfilling, to the last word, My intention." [21] But the official did not understand the significance of the Báb's words. He made no reply and instructed the secretary to follow him. The Báb was then taken from His cell to the houses of the most prominent clergy of the city of Tabriz who, without hesitation, signed the decree for His execution.

Later that morning the Báb was conducted back to the courtyard where a crowd of nearly ten thousand people had gathered to witness His execution. He was delivered into the hands of Sam Khan, the commander of the regiment of soldiers ordered to execute Him. But Sam Khan, finding himself greatly affected by the Báb's behavior, was seized with fear that his action would bring the wrath of God upon him. "I profess the Christian Faith." he explained to the Báb, "and entertain no ill will against you. If your Cause be the Cause of Truth, enable me to free myself from the obligation to shed your blood."

"Follow your instructions." the Báb replied, and if your intention be sincere, the Almighty is surely able to relieve you from your perplexity." 22

Sam Khan ordered his men to drive an iron nail into the wall and attach two ropes to it. From these ropes. the Báb and Anis were suspended. The regiment then arranged itself in three rows, each of two hundred and fifty men. One after the other, each row opened fire. When the smoke from the seven hundred and fifty rifles cleared away, the astonished crowd saw a scene they could hardly believe. Anis was standing before them alive and unhurt, and the Báb had disappeared from sight. The bullets had only cut the ropes from which they had been suspended. A frantic search for the Báb then began. Eventually He was found seated in His cell, completing His interrupted conversation with His secretary. "I have finished my conversation," the Báb said. "Now you may proceed to fulfill your intention." 23

Stunned by what had taken place, Sam Khan refused to allow his men to shoot again and ordered them to leave the courtyard. Another regiment had to be brought in to carry out the execution. Once more the Báb and Anis were suspended in the courtyard, and the soldiers opened fire. This time the bullets found their mark. The bodies of the Báb and Anis were completely shattered; yet their faces remained almost untouched. As the regiment was preparing to open fire, the Báb addressed these final words to the gazing multitude:

"Had you believed in Me, O wayward generation, everyone of you would have followed the example of this youth, who stood in rank above most of you, and willingly would have sacrificed himself in My path. The day will come when you will have recognized Me; that day I shall have ceased to be with you." 24

Nor was this all. The very moment the shots were fired a gale of exceptional violence arose and swept over the city. From noon till night a whirlwind of dust obscured the light of the sun, and blinded the eyes of the people. In Shíráz an "earthquake," foreshadowed in no less weighty a Book than the Revelation of St. John, occurred in 1268 A.H. which threw the whole city into turmoil and wrought havoc amongst its people, a havoc that was greatly aggravated by the outbreak of cholera, by famine and other afflictions. In that same year no less than two hundred and fifty of the firing squad, that had replaced Sám Khán's regiment, met their death, together with their officers, in a terrible earthquake, while the remaining five hundred suffered, three years later, as a punishment for their mutiny, the same fate as that which their hands had inflicted upon the Báb. To insure that none of them had survived, they were riddled with a second volley, after which their bodies, pierced with spears and lances, were exposed to the gaze of the people of Tabríz. The prime instigator of the Báb's death, the implacable Amír-Nizám, together with his brother, his chief accomplice, met their death within two years of that savage act. (Shoghi Effendi – God Passes By p.53-54)

On the evening of the very day of the Báb's execution, which fell on the ninth of July 1850 (28th of Sha'bán 1266 A.H.), during the thirty-first year of His age and the seventh of His ministry, the mangled bodies were transferred from the courtyard of the barracks to the edge of the moat outside the gate of the city. Four companies, each consisting of ten sentinels, were ordered to keep watch in turn over them. On the following morning the Russian Consul in Tabríz visited the spot, and ordered the artist who had accompanied him to make a drawing of the remains as they lay beside the moat. In the middle of the following night a follower of the Báb, Hájí Sulaymán Khán, succeeded, through the instrumentality of a certain Hájí Alláh-Yár, in removing the bodies to the silk factory owned by one of the believers of Mílán, and laid them, the next day, in a specially made wooden casket, which he later transferred to a place of safety. Meanwhile the mullás were boastfully proclaiming from the pulpits that, whereas the holy body of the Immaculate Imám would be preserved from beasts of prey and from all creeping things, this man's body had been devoured by wild animals. No sooner had the news of the transfer of the remains of the Báb and of His fellow-sufferer been communicated to Bahá'u'lláh than He ordered that same Sulaymán Khán to bring them to Tihrán, where they were taken to the Imám-Zádih-Hasan, from whence they were removed to different places, until the time when, in pursuance of 'Abdu'l-Bahá's instructions, they were transferred to the Holy Land, and were permanently and ceremoniously laid to rest by Him in a specially erected mausoleum on the slopes of Mt. Carmel. (Ibid p. 54)

There were tremendous obstacles that 'Abdu'l-Bahá had to overcome to complete His task of depositing the remains of the Báb in God's holy mountain, not the least of which was the long-drawn out negotiations with the shrewd and calculating owner of the site of the Holy Edifice who was demanding an exorbitant price.

"Every stone of that building, every stone of the road leading to it," He, many a time was heard to remark, "I have with infinite tears and at tremendous cost, raised and placed in position." "One night," He, according to an eyewitness, once observed, "I was so hemmed in by My anxieties that I had no other recourse than to recite and repeat over and over again a prayer of the Báb which I had in My possession, the recital of which greatly calmed Me. The next morning the owner of the plot himself came to Me, apologized and begged Me to purchase his property." (Ibid p. 275)

"Finally, ... 'Abdu'l-Bahá brought His undertaking to a successful conclusion, in spite of the incessant machinations of enemies both within and without. On the day of the first Naw-Rúz – March 21st (1909),...... 'Abdu'l-Bahá had the marble sarcophagus transported with great labor to the vault prepared for it, and in the evening, by the light of a single lamp, He laid within it, with His own hands—in the presence of believers from the East and from the West and in circumstances at once solemn and moving—the wooden casket containing the sacred remains of the Báb and His companion." (Ibid p. 276)

"When all was finished, and the earthly remains of the Martyr-Prophet of Shíráz were, at long last, safely deposited for their everlasting rest in the bosom of God's holy mountain, 'Abdu'l-Bahá, Who had cast aside His turban, removed His shoes and thrown off His cloak, bent low over the still open sarcophagus, His silver hair waving about His head and His face transfigured and luminous, rested His forehead on the border of the wooden casket, and, sobbing aloud, wept with such a weeping that all those who were present wept with Him. That night He could not sleep, so overwhelmed was He with emotion." (Ibid p. 276)

"The most joyful tidings is this," He wrote later in a Tablet announcing to His followers the news of this glorious victory, "that the holy, the luminous body of the Báb ... after having for sixty years been transferred from place to place, by reason of the ascendancy of the enemy, and from fear of the malevolent, and having known neither rest nor tranquillity has, through the mercy of the Abhá Beauty, been ceremoniously deposited, on the day of Naw-Rúz, within the sacred casket, in the exalted Shrine on Mt. Carmel..." (Ibid p.276)

"Thus ended a life which posterity will recognize as standing at the confluence of two universal prophetic cycles, the Adamic Cycle stretching back as far as the first dawnings of the world's recorded religious history and the Bahá'í Cycle destined to propel itself across the unborn reaches of time for a period of no less than five thousand centuries. The apotheosis in which such a life attained its consummation marks, as already observed, the culmination of the most heroic phase of the Heroic Age of the Bahá'í Dispensation. It can, moreover, be regarded in no other light except as the most dramatic, the most tragic event transpiring within the entire range of the first Bahá'í century. Indeed it can be rightly acclaimed as unparalleled in the annals of the lives of all the Founders of the world's existing religious systems." (Ibid p. 54-55)

THE LIFE of BAHÁ'U'LLÁH

Bahá'u'lláh, Whose name was Mirza Husayn-'Ali, was born on 12 November 1817 in Tihran, the capital of Persia. His father, Mirza Buzurg, was a distinguished nobleman who held a high-ranking position in the court of the Persian King. "The mother of the Blessed Beauty was so enthralled with Him that she could not contain her amazement at His behaviour. 'This Child never cries,' she would say; 'He is so unlike other Bábí es who cry and scream and are forever restless while in the nursing stage'..."

- 'Abdu'l-Baha (Quoted by Ishraq-Khavari in Risaliy-i-Ayyam-i-Tis'ih p. 62; in 'Stories of Bahá'u'lláh', compiled by Ali-Akbar Furutan)

From an early age, Bahá'u'lláh showed signs of greatness and displayed extraordinary knowledge and wisdom. He did not attend regular school and only received some instruction at home. Regarding His childhood, 'Abdu'l-Baha says:

"The Blessed Perfection, Bahá'u'lláh, belonged to the nobility of Persia. From earliest childhood He was distinguished among His relatives and friends. They said, 'This child has extraordinary power.' In wisdom, intelligence and as a source of new knowledge, He was advanced beyond His age and superior to His surroundings. All who knew Him were astonished at His precocity. It was usual for them to say, 'Such a child will not live,' for it is commonly believed that precocious children do not reach maturity." [1]

In a Tablet, Bahá'u'lláh Himself tells a story from His childhood of the occasion when He attended the wedding celebration of one of His brothers in Tihran. As was the custom in Tihran at that time, a great feast was held for seven days and nights. On the last day, a puppet show about a famous king was performed as entertainment for the guests. Bahá'u'lláh sat in an upper room overlooking the courtyard where a tent had been set up for the performance.

He tells us that the play began with the entrance of a few small figures in human form announcing that the king was approaching. Several more figures then appeared. Some were sweeping, and others were sprinkling water in preparation for the king's arrival. Soon after, the town crier entered the scene and told the people to assemble for an audience with the king. Several groups of figures then made their appearance and took their proper places. Finally, the king made his grand entrance. Wearing a crown on his head, he walked slowly and majestically and seated himself on a throne. Shots were fired; trumpets blasted, and the tent was filled with smoke.

When the smoke cleared, the king, still seated on his throne, was seen surrounded by ministers, princes and state officials, all standing at attention in his presence. At that moment, a thief was brought before the king, who gave the order that he should be beheaded. Without delay, the chief executioner carried out his instructions. After the execution, the king fell into conversation with his ministers and officials. Suddenly news arrived that a rebellion had broken out in one of the frontiers. Troops were immediately dispatched to crush the uprising. A few minutes later, the sound of cannon shot was heard in the background, and it was announced that the king's troops were immediately dispatched to crush the uprising. A few minutes later, the sound of cannon shot was heard in the background, and it was announced that the king's troops were engaged in battle against the rebels.

Thus, the play continued. Bahá'u'lláh was greatly puzzled by the nature of the show. After it was over and the curtain was drawn, He saw a man come out from behind the tent carrying a box under his arm. "What is this box?" Bahá'u'lláh asked him, "and what was the nature of this display?" "All these lavish trappings," he replied, "the king, the princes, and the ministers, their pomp and glory, their might and power, everything you saw, are all now contained within this box."

2 This statement made a great impression on Bahá'u'lláh, and He has declared that:

"Ever since that day, all the trappings of the world have seemed in the eyes of this Youth akin to that same spectacle. They have never been, nor will they ever be, of any weight and consequence, be it to the extent of a grain of mustard seed.... Erelong these outward trappings, these visible treasures, these earthly vanities, these arrayed armies, these adorned vestures, these proud and overweening souls, all shall pass into the confines of the grave, as though into that box. In the eyes of those possessed of insight, all this conflict, contention, and vainglory hath ever been, and will ever be, like unto the play and pastimes of children." 3

Another story associated with Bahá'u'lláh's childhood is related to a dream that His father had in which Bahá'u'lláh appeared to be:

·"... swimming in a vast, limitless ocean. His body shone upon the waters with a radiance that illumined the sea. Around His head, which could distinctly be seen above the waters, there radiated, in all directions, His long, jet-black locks, floating in great profusion above the waves.... a multitude of fishes gathered round Him, each holding fast to the extremity of one hair. Fascinated by the effulgence of His face, they followed Him in whatever direction He swam. Great as was their number, and however firmly they clung to His locks, not one single hair seemed to have been detached from His head, nor did the least injury affect His person. Free and unrestrained, He moved above the waters, and they all followed Him. 4

Impressed by this dream, Bahá'u'lláh's father called a man known for his insight and asked him to interpret it for him. This man, as if inspired by a glimpse of the future glory of Bahá'u'lláh, said:

"The limitless ocean that you have seen in your dream is none other than the world of being. Single-handed and alone, your son will achieve supreme ascendancy over it. Wherever He may please, He will proceed unhindered. No one will resist His march, no one will hinder His progress. The multitude of fishes signifies the turmoil which He will arouse amidst the peoples and kindreds of the earth. Around Him will they gather, and to Him will they cling. Assured of the unfailing protection of the Almighty, this tumult will never harm His person, nor will His loneliness upon the sea of life endanger His safety." [5]

The Divine Manifestations are endowed with innate knowledge and do not need to acquire learning at schools and universities. They are the educators not the educated, Bahá'u'lláh says:

"This Wronged One hath frequented no school, neither hath He attended the controversies of the learned. By My life! Not of Mine own volition have I revealed Myself, but God, of His own choosing, hath manifested Me" [6]

In reference to Bahá'u'lláh's innate knowledge, 'Abdu'I-Baha says:

"No one entered His presence without becoming awe-stricken by His might. The learned men who approached Him were astounded at His knowledge, yet He never attended school nor learned of men. His friends and His family all testify to this, yet His Teachings are the soul of this age.

"The sun emanates from itself and does not draw Its light from other sources. The Divine Teachers have the Innate light; They have knowledge and understanding of all things in the universe; the rest of the world receives Its light from Them and through Them the arts and sciences are revived in each age." [7]

As Bahá'u'lláh grew, the signs of His greatness became increasingly manifest. By the time He was a youth, He was renowned for His keen intelligence, His excellent character, His generosity and compassion. He was capable of solving the most difficult problems and of answering the most complicated and profound questions. Yet despite His extraordinary powers, He never sought position or prominence. When His father passed away, Bahá'u'lláh was asked to follow in his footsteps and assume his position in the court of the King. But He refused. He was not interested in the titles and honors of this world. His interest lay in defending the poor and protecting the needy. At the age of eighteen, Bahá'u'lláh married Asiyih Khanum, and their home became a shelter to all. No one was denied their hospitality.

Bahá'u'lláh was twenty-seven years old when, on 23 May 1844, the Báb declared His Mission to Mulla Husayn in Shiraz. Scarcely three months after that historic event, Bahá'u'lláh received a scroll from the Báb which contained some of His Writings. He instantly testified to the truth of the Báb's Revelation and arose to promote His Teachings. The story of how Bahá'u'lláh came to receive that scroll is as follows.

Soon after the Báb had appointed His chosen disciples, the eighteen Letters of the Living, He called them to His presence and instructed them to spread out and teach His Faith. He gave to each one a special task, assigning to some their own native provinces as the field of their endeavors. Of these eighteen blessed souls, Quddus was chosen to accompany Him on His pilgrimage to Mecca, where He was to proclaim His Mission. To Mulla Husayn, the first to believe in Him, He Addressed these words: "Grieve not that you have not been chosen to accompany Me on My Pilgrimage to Hijaz. I shall, instead, direct your steps to that city which enshrines a Mystery of such transcendent holiness as neither Hijaz nor Shiraz can hope to rival." [8] He gave Mulla Husayn a scroll and instructed him to proceed to Tihran. He told him to beseech God that He would enable him to recognize the splendor of the secret hidden in that city and enter the presence of the Beloved.

Mulla Husayn set out on his mission and, after passing through several cities, arrived in Tihran. There he took a room in a school for religious studies. One of his first acts was to proclaim the Báb's Message to the head of that school, who rejected it with arrogance. However, a young student of the school overheard their conversation and was deeply affected by the words of Mulla Husayn. He decided to visit him at the hour of midnight and learn more about the Message he proclaimed with such enthusiasm. Mulla Husayn received the young man and spoke to him with great courtesy and kindness. He told him that he now understood why he had come to this place. The head of the school had disdainly rejected the Message he had brought. "My hope," said Mulla Husayn, "is that his pupil may, unlike his master, recognize its truth." [9]

During their conversation, Mulla Husayn asked the student where he was from. He replied that he was from the district of Nur, in the province of Mazindaran. "Tell me," inquired Mulla Husayn, "is there today among the family of the late Mirza Buzurg-i-Nuri, who was so renowned for his Character, his charm, and artistic and intellectual attainments, anyone who has proved himself capable of maintaining the high traditions of that illustrious house?" [10]

"Yea," he replied "among his sons now living, one has distinguished Himself by the very traits which characterized His father. By His virtuous life, His high attainments, His loving-kindness and liberality, He has proved Himself a noble descendant of a noble father." "What is His occupation?" asked Mulla Husayn. "He cheers the disconsolate and feeds the hungry." "What of His rank and position?" "He has none apart from befriending the poor and the stranger." "What is His name?" "Husayn-'Ali." [11]

With each answer, Mulla Husayn became more filled with delight. How does He spend His time?" he further asked. "He roams the woods and delights in the beauties of the countryside." "What is His age?"

"Eight and twenty." Mulla Husayn's face was beaming with satisfaction and joy when he asked the young man: "I presume you often meet Him'? "I frequently visit His home," he responded. "Will you deliver into His hands a trust from me?" "Most assuredly," was his reply. Mulla Husayn then handed him the scroll wrapped in a piece of cloth and requested him to present it to Bahá'u'lláh the next day at dawn. "Should He deign to answer me," Mulla Husayn added, "will you be kind enough to acquaint me with His reply?" [12] The student took the scroll and, at daybreak, arose to carry out Mulla Husayn's request.

As he neared the house of Bahá'u'lláh, he saw His brother, Mirza Musa, standing at the gate and explained to him the reason for his visit. Mirza Musa conducted the young man into the presence of Bahá'u'lláh, and the scroll was laid before Him. Bahá'u'lláh asked them to be seated. Unfolding the scroll, He began to read aloud. some of its passages. He had read but a page when He turned to His brother and said: "Musa, what have you to say? Verily I say, whoso believes in the Qu'ran and recognizes its Divine origin, and yet hesitates, though it be for a moment, to admit that these soul-stirring words are endowed with the same regenerating power, has most assuredly erred in his judgment and has strayed far from the path of justice." [13] Dismissing the young man from His presence, Bahá'u'lláh requested him to take to Mulla Husayn, as a gift from Him, a loaf of sugar and a package of tea, and to convey to him His appreciation and love.

Filled with happiness, the young man arose and hurried back to Mulla Husayn. He delivered to him the gift and message from Bahá'u'lláh. No words can describe the joy with which Mulla Husayn received them. With a bowed head, he accepted the gift and fervently kissed it. He then hugged the young man, kissed his eyes, and said: "My dearly beloved friend! I pray that even as you have rejoiced my heart, God may grant you eternal felicity and fill your heart with imperishable gladness." [14] The young man was greatly puzzled by Mulla Husayn's behavior. What could be, he wondered, the nature of the bond that unites these two souls? What could be the cause of fellowship between them? Why should Mulla Husayn have shown such happiness upon receiving so small a gift from Bahá'u'lláh? The young man was faced with a mystery that he could not unravel.

A few days later, Mulla Husayn left for Khurasan, a province in the northeast of Iran. As he said farewell to the young student from Nur, he told him: "Breathe not to anyone what you have heard and witnessed. Let this be a secret hidden within your breast. Divulge not His name, for they who envy His position will arise to harm Him. In your moments of meditation, pray that the Almighty may protect Him, that, through Him, He may exalt the downtrodden, enrich the poor, and redeem the fallen. The secret of things is concealed from our eyes, Ours is the duty to raise the call of the New Day and to proclaim this Divine Message unto all the people. Many a soul will, in this city, shed his blood in this path. That blood will water the Tree of God, will cause it to flourish, and to overshadow all mankind." [15]

The Báb referred to Bahá'u'lláh as "Him Whom God shall make manifest". The Báb's Writings, including His most Holy Book "the Bayan, contain innumerable references in praise of Him Whom God shall make manifest. Below are only a few quotations from the Writings of the Báb to give you a glimpse of the Station of Bahá'u'lláh and the relationship between the Twin Manifestations.

"And know thou of a certainty that by Paradise is meant recognition of and submission unto Him Whom God shall make manifest, and by the fire, the company of such souls as would fail to submit unto Him or to be resigned to His good-pleasure" [16]

"...purge thou thine ear that thou mayest hear no mention besides God, and purge thine eye that it behold naught except God, and thy conscience that it perceive naught other than God, and thy tongue that it proclaim nothing but God, and thy hand to write naught but the words of God, and thy knowledge that it comprehend naught except God, and thy heart that it entertain no wish save God, and in like manner purge all thine acts and thy pursuits that thou mayest be nurtured in the paradise of pure love, and perchance mayest attain the presence of Him Whom God shall make manifest, adorned with a purity which He highly cherisheth, and be sanctified from whosoever hath turned away from Him and doth not support Him." [17]

"Say, verily, the good-pleasure of Him Whom God shall make manifest is the good-pleasure of God, while the displeasure of Him Whom God shall make manifest is none other than the displeasure of God." [18]

From the moment Bahá'u'lláh testified to the truth of the Báb's Revelation, He arose to proclaim it. The first journey He undertook to teach the new Faith was to His ancestral home in Nur, in the province of Mazindaran. There He went to His family home in the village of Takur.

The news of Bahá'u'lláh's arrival in Takur traveled fast throughout the region. Many of the local officials and dignitaries came to greet Him and, at the same time, learn from Him news about the King, his court and the affairs of state. But Bahá'u'lláh responded to their inquiries with little interest. He would quickly change the subject and begin to set forth, in the most eloquent manner; the Message proclaimed by the Báb. His words were so convincing and His statements so sound that all were amazed. Those who heard Him were surprised that a person of His high position would take such a keen interest in matters which usually concerned the clergy and religious leaders. His enthusiasm and depth of knowledge soon attracted large numbers to the new Faith, including many prominent individuals and members of His own family. No one who entered His presence could escape the flow of His sweet words or dared to oppose the truth of His statements, no one except His own uncle.

This uncle did everything possible to discredit Bahá'u'lláh and the truth of the Message He had brought. But when he realized he was incapable of doing so, he went to a well-known Muslim clergyman and pleaded for his assistance. He complained that Bahá'u'lláh had come to Nur and, although not of the clergy, was speaking on religious matters. He warned the theologian that everyone who entered Bahá'u'lláh's presence fell under His spell and was overtaken by the power of His words. "I know not whether he is a sorcerer," he said, "or whether he mixes with his tea some mysterious substance that makes every man who drinks the tea fall a victim to its charm." [19]

Knowing that he could never succeed in challenging Bahá'u'lláh, the theologian ignored the pleas of the uncle. But the Message of the Báb continued to spread like wildfire throughout the district. Alarmed, the followers of the theologian began to put pressure on him to take some form of action, and finally he decided to send his two most outstanding pupils to visit Bahá'u'lláh and investigate the nature of the Message He was propagating. This is the story of what happened when those two representatives entered the presence of Bahá'u'lláh.

'On being told, upon their arrival in Takur, that Bahá'u'lláh had left for His winter home, the representatives of the theologian decided to follow Him there. When they arrived, they found Bahá'u'lláh engaged in revealing a commentary on one of the chapters of the Qur'an. As they sat and listened to Him, they were profoundly impressed by the eloquence of His presentation and the extraordinary manner in which He spoke. One of the representatives, unable to contain himself, arose from his seat and walked to the back of the room and, in an attitude of respect and submissiveness, stood still beside the door. Trembling and with eyes full of tears, he told his companion: "I am powerless to question Bahá'u'lláh. The questions I had planned to ask Him have vanished suddenly from my memory. You are free either to proceed with your inquiry or to return alone to our teacher and inform him of the state in which I find myself. Tell him from me that I can never again return to him. I can no longer forsake this threshold." But the other representative was equally struck by Bahá'u'lláh's words and followed the example of his. friend. "1 have ceased to recognize my teacher," was his reply. "This very moment, I have vowed to God to dedicate the remaining days of my life to the service of Bahá'u'lláh, my true and only Master." [20]

The news of the conversion of the theologian's pupils spread rapidly among the population of Nur. Dignitaries, state officials, religious leaders, traders, and peasants crowded to the presence of Bahá'u'lláh. Hundreds were brought under the banner of the new Faith. No one except Bahá'u'lláh knew, however, that a terrible persecution was soon to follow, a persecution that would tear out by their very roots many of these newly born and tender plants.

What Bahá'u'lláh did in the district of Nur is that which He asks us to do, to arise and teach the Cause of God. Remember that after He accepted the Báb's Revelation, His own first act was to arise and teach hundreds and hundreds of souls.

"O wayfarer in the path of God! Take thou thy portion of the ocean of His grace, and deprive not thyself of the things that lie hidden in its depths. Be thou of them that have partaken of its treasures. A dew drop out of this ocean would, if shed upon all that are in the heavens and on the earth, suffice to enrich them with the bounty of God, the almighty, the All-Knowing, the All-Wise. With the hands of renunciation draw forth from its life-giving waters, and sprinkle therewith all created things, that they may be cleansed from all man-made limitations and may approach the mighty seat of God, this hallowed and resplendent Spot."

"Be not grieved if thou performest it thyself alone. Let God be all-sufficient for thee. Commune intimately with His Spirit and be thou of the thankful. Proclaim the Cause of thy Lord unto all who are in the heavens and on the earth. Should any man respond to thy call, lay bare before him the pearls of the wisdom of the Lord, thy God, which His Spirit hath sent down unto thee, and be thou of them that truly believe. And should any one reject thine offer, turn thou away from him, and put thy trust and confidence in the Lord, they God, the Lord of all worlds."[21]

Divine Revelation is progressive. God reveals His Will progressively through His Manifestations who come from time to time as humanity advances from one stage to another. The same is true of the Revelation of each Manifestation. His Teachings are revealed gradually as the understanding of His followers increases. Oftentimes, even His closest disciples are at first incapable of grasping the full significance of His Revelation. They continue to hold on to the laws and Teachings of the previous religion. Only with time do they come to understand that the new Manifestation is changing some of the laws of the One who came before Him. His purpose is to lay down new laws for humanity's next stage of evolution.

This was the case with the Revelation of the Báb. The Muslims, among whom the Báb appeared, believed that not even a "letter" from the Teachings of the Prophet Muhammad could be changed until the end of the world. Therefore, the Báb allowed His full Message to be made known only gradually. Initially, His sublime Station as the Promised One was not to be openly revealed. His disciples were instructed to spread the glad tidings that the Gate to the Promised One had been opened. Little by little, the person of the Báb became known, but the majority of people were still unaware of His true Station.

During the first years of His Ministry, no changes to the laws of Islam were made. In fact, this was unthinkable to even the closest of His followers. But, as you know, towards the end of His Ministry, while imprisoned in the fortress of Mak-Ku, the Báb revealed a new set of laws in the Persian Bayan. Now was the time for His followers to make a definite break with the past and to proclaim His true Station. This was done at the Conference of Badasht.

Badasht is a village some distance from Tihran in the northeast part of the country. The Conference of Badasht was held in July 1848. Eighty-one of the Báb's most distinguished followers came together in this Conference. The principal participants were Bahá'u'lláh, Quddus and Tahirih.

Although at first Bahá'u'lláh did not appear to have any rank among the Báb's disciples, His role at the Conference was decisive. He rented the gardens in which the Conference was held, and for twenty-two days, all those who had gathered enjoyed His generous hospitality. Each day Bahá'u'lláh revealed a Tablet to be read before the assembled believers. To each He gave a new name. To Tahirih and Quddus He gave the titles by which they will be known throughout history. The title "Tahirih means "the Pure One", and Quddus means "Holy". He Himself was, from that time forward, to be known by the name of Bahá. Later the Báb would reveal a special Tablet for each one of those who had attended the Conference, addressing them by the names they had received on that occasion.

One day Bahá'u'lláh was confined to His bed with illness, and the friends were gathered in His presence. Then, all of a sudden, Tahirih, who was considered the essence of purity and chastity, appeared before them without the veil that, according to the beliefs of Muslims in Iran, all women had to wear in public. Some of the Bábí s present felt that she had brought shame to herself and the new Faith. Quddus was visibly angry. But Tihirih, unshaken and aglow with joy, addressed her companions with eloquence. She called on them to break with the past—-with its religious dogmas, its traditions and ceremonies. The tension that arose between Quddus and Tahirih was eased through Bahá'u'lláh's intervention. While a few of the Báb's followers left the Faith as a result of this proclamation, the majority remained firm and were filled with new enthusiasm. Bahá'u'lláh had masterfully used the occasion to celebrate the dawn of a new Day. Tahirih, through her bold act, had sounded the trumpet-blast announcing the end of the old and the beginning of a new Faith.

The Conference of Badasht also marked the beginning of the most turbulent stage in the development of the Bábí Faith. Soon the persecution of its followers would reach new levels of intensity, and many would be called to martyrdom. It was as if the Conference were a farewell gathering, from where they would go out to perform deeds of great heroism, only to be reunited in the Abba Kingdom.

Those present at the Conference departed together for Mazindaran, but were attacked along the way by the ignorant inhabitants of a village near which the group had stopped to rest. The believers were forced to flee and scattered in different directions. Bahá'u'lláh continued on to Nur in Mazindaran.

News of the Conference of Badasht soon reached Tihran, and the King and his ministers became aware of the events that had taken place and the role played by Bahá'u'lláh at the Conference. The King, weak from an illness that would soon take his life, was advised by the Prime Minister to order the arrest of Bahá'u'lláh. Accordingly, an order was sent to one of the officials of Mazindaran, instructing him to arrest Bahá'u'lláh and bring Him to the capital. As it happened, the order arrived one day before that very official was to give a reception for Bahá'u'lláh, to whom he was devotedly attached. He was greatly distressed and chose not to tell anyone. The next day news reached Mazindaran that the King had died; the arrest order was no longer valid.

The Conference of Badasht marked the shedding of the old and the taking up of the new. The following passage from the Writings of Abdu'l-Baha describes how, from time to time down the ages, the religion of God must be renewed.

"From the seed of reality religion has grown into a tree which has put forth leaves and branches, blossoms and fruit. After a time, this tree has fallen into a condition of decay. The leaves and blossoms have withered and perished; the tree has become stricken and fruitless. It is not reasonable that man should hold to the old tree, claiming that its life forces are undiminished, its fruit unequalled, its existence eternal. The seed of reality must be sown again in human hearts in order that a new tree may grow therefrom and new divine fruits refresh the world. By this means the nations and peoples now divergent in religion will be brought into unity, imitations will be forsaken, and a universal brotherhood in reality itself will be established. Warfare and strife will cease among mankind; all will be reconciled as servants of God. For all are sheltered beneath the tree of His providence and mercy, God is kind to all; He is the giver of bounty to all alike, even as Jesus Christ has declared that God "sendeth rain on the just and on the unjust".——that is to say, the mercy of God is universal. All humanity is under the protection of His love and favor, and unto all He has pointed the way of guidance and progress."[22]

Nasiri'd-Din Shah, the King who rose to the throne in 1848, was far more ruthless than his father, the previous King. From the beginning of his reign, the persecutions of the Bábís increased dramatically. The Báb Himself was martyred in July of 1950 in Tabriz. His oppressed followers, who had witnessed the tragic death of thousands of their fellow believers, had now lost the most Beloved of their hearts. In their thoughts, many blamed the King for the cruelties heaped upon them over the years. But despite these feelings, they continued to be the well-wishers of the government and the people. Their energies were bent on spreading the new Faith through the power of good deeds and convincing arguments. There was, however, a small group, driven by intense anger, who were toying with dangerous ideas. In a state of despair, these foolish few believed that they could change the lot of the Bábí community by attacking tyranny at its root. They began to plot the assassination of the King.

The intentions of the group were communicated to Bahá'u'lláh by one of its leaders. Bahá'u'lláh advised him in the clearest terms that they should give up their plan. He warned them that such an act would bring fresh disasters to the already grief-stricken followers of the Báb. But the plotters were in such a state of bitterness, and the fire of vengeance burned so forcefully in their hearts, that not even the counsels of Bahá'u'lláh were able to stop them. They proceeded to commit an act that forever wilt be considered a stain on the pages of Bábí history, otherwise adorned with nothing but pure, selfless, and heroic deeds.

On 15 August 1852, the King left his summer residence near Tihran on horseback to go for his morning ride. His personal guard moved a few steps ahead of him. There was calmness in the air; all was well for his Majesty. Then, catching everyone by surprise, a young man waiting on the roadside, pretending to be a bystander with a petition to submit to the King, fired a round of shot from his pistol at him. So foolish was this would-be assassin that the pistol he used was charged with bullets which were totally inadequate for the purpose intended. The King was wounded only slightly, but the rage that the attempt on his life created gave the enemies of the Faith an opportunity to excite the people to unimaginable acts of cruelty against the Bábís.

The youth who had shot the King was immediately killed; his body was tied to the tail of a mule and dragged all the way to Tihran, where it was cut into two halves and hung for the public to view. Molten lead was poured down the throat of his companion-this only after he had first been tortured mercilessly yet had refused to give up the names of any of his friends. A third companion was stripped of his clothes, had lighted candles placed into holes made in his flesh, and was paraded before the crowds who shouted and cursed him.

What followed cannot be described in words. The government, the clergy, and their ignorant supporters arose to exterminate the Bábís. The gates to the city were closed, and no one was allowed to leave without being questioned. The Bábís were sought from house to house, arrested and put to death with unmatched cruelty. The following few lines from a letter written by an Austrian officer who was in the King's service give us a glimpse of the horrors of those days. Although reading his words fills us with profound sadness, we do so to be reminded of the sacrifices of the heroic souls who have watered the tree of this Cause with their blood.

"Follow me, my friend, you who lay claim to a heart and European ethics, follow me to the unhappy ones who, with gouged-out eyes, must eat, on the scene of the deed, without any sauce, their own amputated ears; or whose teeth are torn out with inhuman violence by the hand of the executioner; or whose bare skulls are simply crushed by blows from a hammer; or where the bazaar is illuminated with unhappy victims, because on right and left the people dig deep holes in their breasts and shoulders, and insert burning wicks in the wounds. I saw some dragged in chains through the bazaar, preceded by a military band, in whom these wicks had burned so deep that now the fat flickered convulsively in the wound like a newly extinguished lamp. Not seldom it happens that the unwearying ingenuity of the Oriental leads to fresh tortures. They will skin the soles of the Bábí's feet, soak the wounds in boiling oil, shoe the foot like the hoof of a horse, and compel the victim to run. No cry escaped from the victim's breast; the torment is endured in dark silence by the numbed sensation of the fanatic; now he must run; the body cannot endure what the soul has endured; he falls. Give him the *coup de grace!* Put him out of his pain! No! The executioner swings the whip, and-I myself have had to witness it-the unhappy victim of hundredfold tortures runs! This is the beginning of the end. As for the end itself, they hang the scorched and perforated bodies by their hands and feet to a tree head downwards, and now every Persian may try his marksmanship to his heart's content from a fixed but not too proximate distance on the noble quarry placed at his disposal I saw corpses torn by nearly one hundred and fifty bullets.....When I read over again what I have written I am overcome by the thought that those who are with you in our dearly beloved Austria may doubt the full truth of the picture and accuse me of exaggeration. Would to God that I had not lived to see it! But by the duties of my profession I was unhappily often, only too often, a witness of these abominations. At present I never leave my house, in order not to meet with fresh scenes of horror ... Since my whole soul revolts against such infamy ... I will no longer maintain my connection with the scene of such crimes." [23]

On the day that the attempt on the life of the King took place, Bahá'u'lláh was the guest of the Prime Minister's brother in a village near Tihrin. The news of the calamity soon reached Him, and He was advised to hide until the storm had passed. The mother of the King blamed Bahá'u'lláh for the attempt on her son's life and was demanding His arrest. But Bahá'u'lláh refused to go into hiding; on the contrary, the next day, He mounted His horse and rode towards the headquarters of the King. The King and his court were astonished to learn of Bahá'u'lláh's approach. How could someone who was being accused of such a terrible crime, far from running away ride so confidently towards danger? The King immediately ordered Bahá'u'lláh's arrest. The efforts of some of His friends who tried to find a refuge for Him in the house of the Prime Minister failed. He was arrested in the village of Shimiran, some 30 kilometers from the capital, and put in chains.

On foot and exposed to the fierce rays of the midsummer sun, Bahá'u'lláh was brought from Shimiran to Tihran. The crowds, who had been told He was the enemy of their King, shouted abuses at Him all along the route. The story of the old woman who wished to throw a stone at Him as He approached the dungeon which was to be the place of His imprisonment captures the madness of the crowd on that day and demonstrates the love that was in His heart as He faced the most grievous of calamities.

As He was nearing that dungeon, an old and feeble woman was seen forcing her way through the crowd with a stone in her hand, eager to throw it in the face of Bahá'u'lláh. She had a look of determination and fanaticism which few women her age could muster. Her whole body shook with rage as she stepped forward and raised her hand preparing to cast her stone. "I adjure you," she pleaded, as she ran after those conducting Bahá'u'lláh to the dungeon, "give me a chance to fling my stone in his face!" "Suffer not this woman to be disappointed," were Bahá'u'lláh's words to His guards, as He saw her rushing towards Him, "Deny her not what she regards as a meritorious act in the sight of God." [24]

Throughout His life, Bahá'u'lláh was surrounded by enemies seeking to harm Him. But never did He try to conceal Himself; never did He protect Himself. On the contrary, at all times He was visible before the eyes of men and withstood with serenity and calm the attacks of those who opposed Him. Although they were determined to extinguish His light, they were unable to do so, and day by day His splendor grew more radiant.

"Not even for a single moment hath this Wronged One ever concealed Himself. Rather hath He at all times remained steadfast and conspicuous before the eyes of all men. Never have We retreated, nor shall We ever seek flight. In truth it is the foolish people who flee from Our presence....Praise be to God! The Cause whereof this Wronged One is the Bearer standeth as high as heaven and shineth resplendent as the sun. Concealment hath no access unto this station, nor is there any occasion for fear or silence." [25]

"Unveiled and unconcealed, this Wronged One hath, at all times, proclaimed before the face of all the peoples of the world that which will serve as the key for unlocking the doors of sciences, of arts, of knowledge of well-being, of prosperity and wealth. Neither have the wrongs inflicted by the oppressors succeeded in silencing the shrill voice of the Most Exalted Pen, nor have the doubts of the perverse or the seditious been able to hinder Him from revealing the Most Sublime Word." [26]

Siya-Chal, the name of the prison to which Bahá'u'lláh was taken on that calamitous day, means the "Black Pit". Originally a reservoir of water for one of the public baths in Tihran, it was at that time an underground dungeon in which criminals of the worst type were confined.

To reach the prison one was taken through a pitch-black passageway and then down three steep flights of stairs. The dungeon was wrapped in thick darkness. There were no windows or outlets, other than the passage through which one entered. Nearly one hundred and fifty prisoners—thieves, murderers and highwaymen—were crowded into this dark, icy-cold space. The floor was covered with dirt and filth and crawling with insects. Most of the prisoners did not have clothes or even a cover to lie on. The smell was foul beyond belief.

Under these cruel conditions Bahá'u'lláh and a number of Bábí s were imprisoned by the King. Bahá'u'lláh's feet were put in stocks, and a heavy chain weighing some 50 kilograms was placed around His neck. For the first three days and nights they were given nothing to eat or drink. The family of Bahá'u'lláh would prepare food for Him and ask the guards to bring it to Him. Although at first they refused, they gradually gave in to their pleas. But, even then, no one could be sure whether the food reached Him, or whether He would accept to eat it while His fellow-prisoners went hungry.

Bahá'u'lláh and His companions, also in stocks and chains, all huddled together in one cell. They had been placed in two rows, each facing the other. Bahá'u'lláh taught them to repeat certain verses which, every night, they chanted with great fervor. "God is sufficient unto me; He verily is the All-sufficing," one row would chant, and the other would reply: "In Him let the trusting trust." Into the early hours of the morning, the chorus of their happy voices could be heard. So strong was their melody that it reached the ears of the King, whose palace was not far from the Siyah-Chal. "What means this sound?" he was reported to have asked. "It is the anthem the Bábís are intoning in their prison," [27] was the reply. The King fell silent.

Every day, the jailors would enter the cell and would call out the name of one of the Bábís, ordering him to arise and follow them to the foot of the gallows. With eagerness, the owner of the name would respond to that call. His chains removed, he would jump to his feet and, in a state of uncontrollable delight, would approach Bahá'u'lláh and embrace Him. He would then embrace each of his fellow-prisoners and would go forth, with a heart filled with hope and joy, to meet the death that awaited him. Soon after the martyrdom of each of these heroic souls, the executioner, who had grown to admire Bahá'u'lláh, would come to Him and would inform Him of the circumstances of the death of the martyr and of the joy with which he had endured, to the very end, the pain inflicted upon him.

The terrible conditions under which Bahá'u'lláh and His companions were imprisoned in the Siyah-Chal have been described by Bahá'u'lláh in His own Words about the days spent in that dark dungeon. In one passage He says:

"Upon Our arrival We were first conducted along a pitch-black corridor, from whence We descended three steep flights of stairs to the place of confinement assigned to Us. The dungeon was wrapped in thick darkness, and Our fellow prisoners numbered nearly a hundred and fifty souls: thieves, assassins and highwaymen. Though crowded, it had no other outlet than the passage by which We entered. No pen can depict that place, nor any tongue describe Its loathsome smell. Most of these men had neither clothes nor bedding to lie on. God alone knoweth what befell Us in that most foul-smelling and gloomy place!"[28]

Nabil, the immortal historian of the Baha'i Faith, recounts the words he himself heard from Bahá'u'lláh:

"All those who were struck down by the storm that raged during that memorable year in Tihran were Our fellow prisoners in the Siyah-Chal, where We were confined. We were all huddled together in one cell, our feet in stocks, and around our necks fastened the most galling of chains. The air we breathed was laden with the foulest impurities, while the floor on which we sat was covered with filth and infested with vermin. No ray of light was allowed to penetrate that pestilential dungeon or to warm Its icy coldness. We were placed in two rows, each facing the other. We had taught them to repeat certain verses which, every night, they chanted with extreme fervor. 'God is sufficient unto me; He verily is the All-sufficing!' one row would intone, while the other would reply: 'In Him let the trusting trust.' The chorus of these gladsome voices would continue to peal out until the early hours of the morning....

"Every day Our jailors, entering Our cell, would call the name of one of Our companions, bidding him arise and follow them to the foot of the gallows. With what eagerness would the owner of that name respond to that solemn call! Relieved of his chains, he would spring to bis feet and, in a state of uncontrollable delight, would approach and embrace Us. We would seek to comfort him with the assurance of an everlasting life in the world beyond, and, filling his heart with hope and joy, would send him forth to win the crown of glory. He would embrace, in turn, the rest of his fellow-prisoners and then proceed to die as dauntlessly as he had lived. Soon after the martyrdom of each of these companions, We would be informed by the executioner, who had grown to be friendly to Us, of the circumstances of the death of his victim, and of the joy with which he had endured his sufferings to the very end."[29]

'There is a profound concept which every student of history must understand, namely, that the Cause of God advances through a series of crises and victories. The forces of ignorance, injustice, cruelty, and fanaticism continually attack the Baha'i community and give rise to crises. But each time, in accordance with the Will of God, the forces of darkness are defeated, and the result is a victory. The Cause moves from crisis to victory to crisis to victory, and no power on earth is capable of stopping its onward march.

The short Ministry of the Báb had already followed such a course. The ordinary observer, however, would have assumed that the latest crisis could not be overcome: The Báb had been martyred. Thousands of His followers had been killed in a massacre of untold cruelty. The most outstanding of His disciples had been martyred, and the only One Who could revive hope was under chains in the darkest of dungeons. The crisis was indeed profound, but the victory that followed was most glorious.

In the Siyah-Chal, God made known to Bahá'u'lláh the greatness of His Station. Wrapped in gloom, breathing the foulest of air, His feet in stocks, and His neck weighed down by a mighty chain, Bahá'u'lláh received the first intimations of God's Revelation within His soul. Under these dreadful circumstances, the "Most Great Spirit" revealed itself to Him, bidding Him to arise and speak forth the Word of God.

At times, He would feel as if something flowed from the crown of His head over His breast, as a mighty torrent falls upon the earth from the summit of a high mountain. He saw the Maiden of Heaven suspended before Him, speaking to His inner and outer being, referring to Him as the Best-Beloved of the worlds, the Beauty of God, and the power of God's sovereignty. He was assured that He would be made victorious by Himself and by His Pen, and by the aid of those whom God would raise up.

Thus, out of the darkness of the Black Pit rose the Sun of Truth. The Báb's promise had been fulfilled. The Baha'i Revelation was born. Yet Bahá'u'lláh did not inform anyone of what had occurred. He would await the appointed hour ordained by God, to make His Mission known.

Humanity is fortunate to have this most momentous occurrence in religious history recorded in Bahá'u'lláh's own Words. Calling to mind the way God's Revelation first filled His soul, He says:

"One night in a dream, these exalted words were heard on every side: 'Verily. We shall render Thee victorious by Thyself and by Thy Pen. Grieve Thou not for that which hath befallen Thee, neither be Thou afraid, for Thou art in safety. Erelong will God raise up the treasures

of the earth ·—men who will aid Thee through Thyself and through
Thy Name, wherewith God hath revived the hearts of such as have
recognized Him. ' " 30

In another passage He describes the effect of God's Revelation on
His being:

"During the days I lay in the prison of Tihran, though the galling
weight of the chains and the stench-filled air allowed Me but little
sleep, still in those infrequent moments of slumber I felt as if something
flowed from the crown of My head over My breast, even as a mighty
torrent that precipitateth itself upon the earth from the summit of a
lofty mountain. Every limb of My body would, as a result, be set afire.
At such moments my tongue recited what no man could bear to hear."
31

Yet in another passage He describes how the Maiden, symbolizing
the "Most Great Spirit"; appeared to Him:

"While engulfed in tribulations I heard a most wondrous, a most
sweet voice, calling above My head. Turning My face, I beheld a
Maiden—-the embodiment of the remembrance of the name of My
Lord—-suspended in the air before Me. So rejoiced was she in her
very soul that her countenance shone with the ornament of the
good-pleasure of God, and her cheeks glowed with the brightness of
the All-Merciful. Betwixt earth and heaven, she was raising a call which
captivated the hearts and minds of men. She was imparting to both My
inward and outer being tidings which rejoiced My soul, and the souls
of God's honored servants. Pointing with her finger unto My head, she
addressed all who are in heaven and all who are on earth, saying: 'By
God! This is the Best-Beloved of the worlds, and yet ye comprehend
not. This is the Beauty of God amongst you, and the power of His
sovereignty within you, could ye but understand. This is the Mystery of
God and His Treasure, the Cause of God, and His glory unto all who

are in the kingdoms of Revelation and of creation, if ye be of them that perceive.'" [32]

So important is the concept of crisis and victory that it is worthwhile to pause and reflect on the power of the Cause, which overcomes every obstacle in its path. To help do so, here are some quotations below-one from the Writings of Bahá'u'lláh and the other from a letter written on behalf of Shoghi Effendi, the grandson of Bahá'u'lláh and the Guardian of the Cause.

"Behold how in this Dispensation the worthless and foolish have fondly imagined that by such instruments as massacre, plunder and banishment they can extinguish the Lamp which the Hand of Divine power hath lit, or eclipse the Day Star of everlasting splendor. How utterly unaware they seem to be of the truth that such adversity is the oil that feedeth the flame of this Lamp! Such is God's transforming power. He changeth whatsoever He willeth; He verily hath power over all things...'" [33]

""This Cause, as every Divine Cause, cannot be effectively established unless it encounters and valiantly triumphs over the forces of opposition with which it is assailed. The history of the Faith is in itself a sufficient proof of that. Trials and persecutions have always been, and will continue to be, the lot of the chosen ones of God. But these they should consider as blessings in disguise, as through them their faith will be quickened, purified, and strengthened. Bahá'u'lláh compares such afflictive trials to the oil which feeds the lamp of the Cause of God." [34]

While Bahá'u'lláh remained under chains in the Siyah-Chal, His enemies were busy trying to obtain His death sentence from the King. Bahá'u'lláh, however, was loved by people high and low alike and could not be executed so easily. Proof was needed that would connect Him with the attempt on the King's life. But the more they tried to find proof, the more it became evident that He was entirely innocent.

Unable to prove guilt, these ruthless enemies decided to poison His food. So strong was the poison, however, that its initial effects were quickly noticed, and Bahá'u'lláh stopped eating the poisonous meal they had offered Him. In the end, the authorities had no other choice but to release Him from prison, but this they did only on the condition that he would leave the country and go into exile.

Bahá'u'lláh had endured four months in prison. He was now ill and exhausted. The inhumane conditions of the prison, the chain of some 50 kilos around His neck, and finally the poison, had left Him in such a weakened state that He was confined to His bed under watchful care. The links of the chain had made deep wounds in His neck and although these healed with time, the scars remained until the end of His life. In the midst of all this, the family had to prepare to undertake an arduous journey within one-months' time. Bahá'u'lláh had been given the freedom to choose the place of His exile. He chose Baghdad, then a city in the Ottoman Empire and today the capital of Iraq.

The trip lasted from 12 January 1853 to 8 April of the same year. It was the middle of winter, and Bahá'u'lláh and His family had to travel through the western part of Iran where winters are bitterly cold. The supplies they had for the journey were not sufficient, and they had to be content with little food. But the Protector of this small band of travelers was Almighty God Himself, and through His unfailing assistance, they arrived safely in Baghdad.

Iran had deprived itself of the bounty of the presence of Bahá'u'lláh and had forced Him to leave, never to return to His native land. 'Iraq was now to be the home of the most precious Being on the planet. An outstanding Baha'i historian has these words to say about Bahá'u'lláh's exile from Iran:

"As Bahá'u'lláh neared the frontier, a period drew to its close. Were the people of Iran aware of the loss they sustained? Steeped in ignorance, sunk in bigotry, blinded by prejudice, led by self-seeking men, beguiled by falsehoods, theirs was not to see and know. And thus the Redeemer of the world passed out of their midst. He Who once was loved and respected by rich and poor, high and low, prince and peasant alike, was now deserted by the same people on whom He had lavished mercy, love, justice and charity at all times. Iran lost the presence of Bahá'u'lláh, but could His spirit ever be absent from that or any other land?" [35]

The following prayer revealed by Bahá'u'lláh will help you get a glimpse of the suffering He experienced in the Siyah-Chal and the hardships He endured in the months immediately after.

"My God, My Master, My Desire!... Thou hast created this atom of dust through the consummate power of Thy might, and nurtured Him with Thine hands which none can chain up... The throat Thou didst accustom to the touch of silk Thou hast, in the end, clasped with strong chains, and the body Thou didst ease with brocades and velvets Thou hast at last subjected to the abasement of a dungeon. Thy decree hath shackled Me with unnumbered fetters, and cast about My neck chains that none can sunder. A number of years have passed during which afflictions have, like showers of mercy, rained upon Me... How many the nights during which the weight of chains and fetters allowed Me no rest, and how numerous the days during which peace and tranquility were denied Me, by reason of that wherewith the hands and tongues of men have afflicted Me! Both bread and water which Thou hast, through Thine all-embracing mercy, allowed unto the beasts of the field, they have, for a time, forbidden unto this servant, and the things they refused to inflict upon such as have seceded from Thy Cause, the same have they suffered to be inflicted upon Me, until, finally, Thy decree was irrevocably fixed, and Thy behest summoned this servant to depart out of Persia, accompanied by a number of frail-bodied men and children of tender age, at this time when the cold is so intense that one cannot even speak, and ice and snow so abundant that it is impossible to move." [36]

In Baghdad, Bahá'u'lláh, rented a house in the old quarter of the city. In the months following His arrival, an increasing number of Bábís made their way to Baghdad. Unfortunately, many had sunk into a pitiful state; they were confused and bewildered, and some were committing acts unworthy of a follower of the Báb. Bahá'u'lláh received all these who arrived with boundless love and assisted them in cleansing their hearts and in reviving their spirits. Under His influence, the fortunes of the Bábí community began to change, and hope blossomed again. But alas, a new crisis was in the making. This time its source was within the community itself; the cause of misfortune was none other than Bahá'u'lláh's own half-brother, Mirza Yahya, who claimed to be the Báb's successor.

In reality, the Báb had not seen the need to name a successor, for He knew that the Promise of All Ages would soon appear. What He had done was to nominate, on the advice of Bahá'u'lláh and another disciple, Mirza Yahya as a figure-head. This would enable Bahá'u'lláh to promote the Cause in relative security. Mizra Yahya had received much love and support from Bahá'u'lláh throughout his life, yet he was both ambitious and cowardly. The martyrdom of the Báb had shocked him to such an extent that he had almost lost his faith. He had wandered for a while as a dervish in the mountains of Mazindaran, his behavior so shameful that he had driven some of the Bábís of the region away from the Cause. Using one disguise after another, he had finally come to Baghdad, and having obtained a sum of money from Bahá'u'lláh in order to engage in commerce, was living under a new name in one of the neighborhoods of the city.

The growing respect and love being shown to Bahá'u'lláh by the followers of the Báb, as well as His rising prestige among the city officials, had a terrible effect on Mirza Yahya. His jealousy was aroused, and its fire burned with such intensity that it consumed every trace of decency. Together with an associate more shameless than himself, Mirza Yahya set out to sow the seeds of doubt among the Bábís about

Bahá'u'lláh's intentions. Once again, the clouds of suspicion, fear and idle fancy descended upon the Bábí community. The short period of calm and tranquility had come to an end and, day by day, Bahá'u'lláh's sufferings were intensifying.

On the morning of 10 April 1854, Bahá'u'lláh's family woke to find that He was gone. He had left the city without telling anyone His purpose or destination. Seeing where the actions of Mirza Yahya were leading, Bahá'u'lláh had chosen to retire to the mountains of Kurdistan, northeast of Baghdad. "The one object of Our retirement", He Himself has later said, was to avoid becoming the object of discord among the faithful, a source of disturbance unto Our companions, the means of injury to any soul, or the cause of sorrow to any heart."[37]

In the wilderness, some distance from the town of Sulaymaniyyih, Bahá'u'lláh lived alone in communion with God. He was content with little food. At times He received some milk from the shepherds in the surrounding area and occasionally, visited the town to obtain the minimum necessities of life. Yet, even during these brief contacts with the people of the region, Bahá'u'lláh's greatness could not be kept hidden from their eyes. His love and wisdom attracted the inhabitants of Sulaymaniyyih and His fame began to spread to the neighboring areas. News of a man of extraordinary wisdom and eloquence living in that region of Kurdistan finally reached Bagdad. His family, realizing that this Personage could be none other than Bahá'u'lláh, sent a trusted believer to beg Him to return. Bahá'u'lláh accepted their request thus ending His two-year voluntary withdrawal.

Every Manifestation of God makes a Covenant with His followers. The followers of the Báb had entered into a Covenant with Him to seek and accept Him Whom God would make manifest and to live in obedience to His commands. Although Bahá'u'lláh had not yet told them that He was the One promised by the Báb, His greatness was becoming more and more apparent with each passing day, and a few had even begun to recognize His Station. Mirza Yahya was not blind to Bahá'u'lláh's majesty and glory. But his jealousy and ambition were aroused, causing him to engage in mischief which would finally lead him to openly break the Covenant of the Báb. Referring to the turmoil and tribulations which were awaiting them, Bahá'u'lláh warned the friends:

"The days of tests are now come. Oceans of dissension and tribulation are surging, and the Banners of Doubt are, in every nook and corner, occupied in stirring up mischief and in leading men to perdition.... Suffer not the voice of some of the soldiers of negation to cast doubt into your midst, neither allow yourselves to become heedless of Him Who is the Truth, inasmuch as in every Dispensation such contentions have been raised. God, however, will establish His Faith, and manifest His light albeit the stirrers of sedition abhor it.... Watch ye every day for the Cause of God.... All are held captive in His grasp. No place is there for anyone to flee to. Think not the Cause of God to be a thing lightly taken, in which any one can gratify his whims. In various quarters a number of souls have, at the present time, advanced this same claim. The time is approaching when...every one of them will have perished and been lost, nay will have come to naught and become a thing unremembered, even as the dust itself" [38]

During Bahá'u'lláh's absence, the fortunes of the Faith had reached the lowest point in its history. As expected, Mirza Yahya had proved himself to be incapable of leading oven the small community in Baghdad. In various parts, a number of the Bábís were engaged in activities that brought shame to the precious Cause of the Báb. So, once again, Bahá'u'lláh took on the task of reviving the community. His arrival in March 1856 was announced to the believers, and His door was opened to all who longed for truth. The modest residence in which He lived with His family became the center wherein gathered seekers, visitors and pilgrims. Everyone who came into His presence was transformed by the power of His sweet and loving words. Those who had the bounty of living in close proximity to Him felt as if they were in paradise. They became a new creation, utterly detached from the things of this world. This is how Nabil, the great historian of the early Baha'i Era, has described the state of those souls:

"Many a night no less than ten persons subsisted on no more than a pennyworth of dates. No one knew to whom actually belonged the shoes, the cloaks, or the robes that were to be found in their houses. Whoever went to the bazaar could claim that the shoes upon their feet were his own, and each one who entered the presence of Bahá'u'lláh could affirm that the cloak and robe he then wore belonged to him. Their own names they had forgotten, their hearts were emptied of aught else except adoration for their Beloved....O, for the joy of those days, and the gladness and wonder of those hours!" [39]

Bahá'u'lláh remained in Baghdad for seven years following His return from Sulaymaniyyih. During this time, He continued to keep hidden His Station as the Manifestation of God for this Day. Yet Divine love poured out from Him in such measure that receptive hearts could not but be touched by it. The Divine guidance He revealed in conversations and in written verses and tablets transformed the character of the Bábís who had been left shepherdless for so many years. These are the years during which He revealed the Book of Certitude, wherein He explained the nature of God's Revelation in such clear terms that the foundations of man-made dogmas of the past were destroyed. It is during this same period that He revealed, as He walked the banks of river Tigris wrapped in meditation, the Hidden Words, so cherished as a guide to our spiritual growth. The rapidity with which revealed verses flowed from His Pen was astonishing. This is how He Himself has referred to that period of extraordinary potency:

"... We revealed, as a copious rain, by the aid of God and His Divine Grace and mercy, Our verses, and sent them to various parts of the world. We exhorted all men, and particularly this people, through Our wise counsels and loving admonitions, and forbade them to engage in sedition, quarrels, disputes and conflict. As a result of this, and by the grace of God, waywardness and folly were changed into piety and understanding, and weapons converted into instruments of peace" [40]

The opening passages from the Book of Certitude and the Hidden Words are as follows: The Book of Certitude opens thus:

"No man shall attain the shores of the ocean of true understanding except he be detached from all that is in heaven and on earth. Sanctify your souls, O ye peoples of the world, that haply ye may attain that station which God hath destined for you and enter thus the tabernacle which, according to the dispensations of Providence, hath been raised in the firmament of the Bayan." [41]

And the opening passage of the Hidden Words reads:

"This is that which hath descended from the realm of glory, uttered by the tongue of power and might, and revealed unto the Prophets of old. We have taken the inner essence thereof and clothed it in the garment of brevity, as a token of grace unto the righteous, that they may stand faithful unto the Covenant of God, may fulfill in their lives His trust, and in the realm of spirit obtain the gem of divine virtue." [42]

The seven years of Bahá'u'lláh's life in Baghdad represent a period of magnificent victories. It was to be expected, then, that sooner or later a crisis should arise, which in turn would be followed by an even greater victory. The growing prestige of Bahá'u'lláh did not go unnoticed by the enemies of the Faith. The most active among them was a certain Shaykh who used every means at his disposal to convince the officials of both the Persian and Ottoman Governments, as well as the clergy, to rise in opposition against Him. But for years the Shaykh's efforts were frustrated by Bahá'u'lláh's wisdom and the nobility of His words and deeds.

One time, for example, this Shaykh called together the most distinguished clergy in the region with the intention of obtaining their unanimous condemnation of Bahá'u'lláh. All were prepared to launch an attack against the small band of exiles in Baghdad in order to destroy the Faith at its heart. To their surprise, however, the most highly placed among them, a man known for his justice and piety, refused to give the necessary sentence against the Bábís. He told the group that, to his knowledge, the Bábí community had done nothing that would justify such an act and left the gathering.

Since its original plan failed, the group decided to send a learned man to Bahá'u'lláh and to submit to Him a number of questions in order to test His knowledge. When Bahá'u'lláh replied to all the questions, this messenger accepted, on behalf of the group of clergy, the vastness of His knowledge. But then, he said, in order to satisfy everyone concerned of the truth of His Mission, He should perform a miracle for them. "Although you have no right to ask this," Bahá'u'lláh replied, "for God should test His creatures, and they should not test God, still l allow and accept this request." [43] He told the messenger, however, that first the clergy should choose one miracle and write down that, after its performance, they would no longer have any doubts about Him and they would all recognize Him and would confess the truth of His Cause. They should seal this document and bring it to Him.

This clear and challenging reply affected the messenger profoundly. He instantly arose, kissed the knee of Bahá'u'lláh, and departed. He delivered Bahá'u'lláh's message to the group of clergy. They debated over it for three days, but could not come to any decision. Finally, they had no other choice but to drop the matter.

But these ruthless enemies of the Faith did not give up their schemings against Bahá'u'lláh. They continued to stir up mischief and to misrepresent His intentions to the authorities, until at last, in the spring of 1863, their efforts yielded fruit, and the next crisis appeared.

Towards the end of His stay in Baghdad, Bahá'u'lláh began to make occasional reference to the tests and trials that would lie ahead. A dream He once related to the friends caused them great distress. "I saw," He wrote in a Tablet, "the Prophets and the Messengers gather and seat themselves around Me, moaning, weeping and loudly lamenting. Amazed, I inquired of them the reason, whereupon their lamentation and weeping waxed greater, and they said unto Me: 'We weep for Thee, O Most Great Mystery, O Tabernacle of Immortality!' They wept with such a weeping that I too wept with them. Thereupon the Concourse on high addressed Me saying:'.... Erelong shalt Thou behold with Thine own eyes what no Prophet hath beheld... Be patient, be patient.'...they continued addressing Me the whole night until the approach of dawn."[44]

Early in the spring of 1863, during the twelve-day festival of Naw-Ruz marking the Persian new year Bahá'u'lláh revealed the Tablet of the Holy Mariner which, in a mystical language, foretold future events and spoke of betrayal and separation. This Tablet was read to the friends gathered in His presence on 26 March. Oceans of sorrow surged in their hearts as they sensed that Bahá'u'lláh was to be taken from them. That very day, a messenger delivered to Bábá'u'llah a communication requesting an interview between Him and the Governor of Baghdad. On the following day, Bahá'u'lláh was presented with a letter from the Prime Minister of the Ottoman Empire to the Governor, worded in a courteous manner, inviting Bahá'u'lláh to travel to the Ottoman capital, Constantinople (Istanbul today). A mounted escort was ordered to accompany Him for His protection. Bahá'u'lláh agreed to the request at once but refused to accept the money that the government was offering for His travels. The Governor's representative insisted He accept it, saying that the authorities would be offended if He did not do so. Finally. He took the generous sum and immediately distributed it among the poor of the city.

News of Bahá'u'lláh's exile from Baghdad shook the Bábí community. The friends were overwhelmed with sadness, and, at first, no one was able to sleep or eat. Gradually, however, they were calmed through Bahá'u'lláh's kind and tender words and accepted that most would be deprived of the bounty of accompanying Him on the next stage of His exile. As a token of His love, He wrote in His own handwriting a Tablet for each of the friends who lived in the city—man, woman, and child.

In the vicinity of Baghdad, there was a beautiful garden full of roses, and the rose was Bahá'u'lláh's favorite flower. On the morning of 22 April 1863, He left the city and entered the garden. The believers., and indeed vast numbers of the people of Baghdad, were grief stricken. The Bábí community, now totally revived through the tender care of Bahá'u'lláh, had entered yet another crisis. What would be the future of this young Faith whose only Hope was being exiled to a place so far away from the majority of its adherents? The answer awaiting those heartbroken Bábís who gathered to bid Him farewell was stupendous. Bahá'u'lláh would tear away the veils that hid His true Station from the eyes of men and would openly declare that He was the Promised One of all ages.

Bahá'u'lláh stayed in the garden known today as the Garden of Ridvan, for twelve days before departing for Constantinople. His enemies had tried to strike a fatal blow at His Cause by separating Him from the majority of the believers. God, however turned the farewell into an occasion of immense joy. The declaration of His Mission created new life in the souls of His companions. This was the Day of Days for which the Báb had prepared them. Bahá'u'lláh Himself has said that on that Day "all created things were immersed in the sea of purification". [45]

Unfortunately, there is little known of the details of the conversations Bahá'u'lláh held with the stream of visitors He received in the Garden of Ridvan. The following words of the historian Nabil give us only a glimpse of the glory of those days:

"Every day, ere the hour of dawn, the gardeners would pick the roses which lined the four avenues of the garden, and would pile them in the center of the floor of His blessed tent. So great would be the heap that when His companions gathered to drink their morning tea in His presence, they would be unable to see each other across it. All these roses Bahá'u'lláh would, with His own hands, entrust to those whom He dismissed from His presence every morning to be delivered, on His behalf, to His Arab and Persian friends in the city....One night, the ninth night of the waxing moon, I happened to be one of those who watched beside His blessed tent. As the hour of midnight approached, I saw Him issue from His tent, pass by the places where some of His companions were sleeping, and begin to pace up and down the moonlit, flower-bordered avenues of the garden. So loud was the singing of the nightingales on every side that only those who were near Him could hear distinctly His voice. He continued to walk until, pausing in the midst of one of these avenues, He observed: 'Consider these nightingales. So great is their love for these roses, that sleepless from dusk till dawn, they warble their melodies and commune with burning passion with the object of their adoration. How then can those who claim to be afire with the rose-like beauty of the Beloved choose to sleep?' For three successive nights I watched and circled round His blessed tent. Every time I passed by the couch whereon He lay, I would find Him wakeful, and every day, from morn till eventide, I would see Him ceaselessly engaged in conversing with the stream of visitors who kept flowing in from Baghdad. Not once could I discover in the words He spoke any trace of dissimulation." [46]

Today, the Baha'is of the world celebrate the twelve days from 21 April to 2 May as the Festival of Ridvan, the holiest and most significant of all Baha'i festivals. The following are passages from a Tablet revealed by Bahá'u'lláh. They call to mind Bahá'u'lláh's Declaration in the Garden of Ridvan.

"The Divine Springtime is come, O Most Exalted Pen, for the Festival of the All-Merciful is fast approaching. Bestir thyself, and magnify, before the entire creation, the name of God, and celebrate His praise, in such wise that all created things may be regenerated and made new. Speak, and hold not thy peace. The day star of blissfulness shineth above the horizon of Our name, the Blissful, inasmuch as the kingdom of the name of God hath been adorned with the ornament of the name of thy Lord, the Creator of the heavens. Arise before the nations of the earth and arm thyself with the power of this Most Great Name, and be not of those who tarry....

"Canst thou discover any one but Me, O Pen, in this Day? What hath become of the creation and the manifestations thereof? What of the names and their Kingdom? Whither are gone all created things, whether seen or unseen? What of the hidden secrets of the universe and its revelations? Lo, the entire creation hath passed away! Nothing remaineth except My Face, the Ever-Abiding, the Resplendent, the All-Glorious.

"This is the Day whereon naught can be seen except the splendors of the Light that shineth from the face of Thy Lord, the Gracious, the Most Bountiful. Verily, We have caused every soul to expire by virtue of Our irresistible and all-subduing sovereignty. We have, then, called into being a new creation, as a token of Our grace unto men. I am, verily, the All-Bountiful, the Ancient of Days....

"Say: This is the Paradise on whose foliage the wine of utterance hath imprinted the testimony: 'He that was hidden from the eyes of men is revealed, girded with sovereignty and power!' This is the Paradise, the rustling of whose leaves proclaims: 'O ye that inhibit the heavens and the earth! There hath appeared what hath never previously appeared. He Who, from everlasting, had concealed His Face from the sight of creation is now come.' From the whispering breeze that wafteth amidst its branches there cometh the cry: 'He Who is the sovereign Lord of all is made manifest. The Kingdom is God's,' while from its streaming waters can be heard the murmur: 'All eyes are gladdened, for He Whom none hath beheld, Whose secret no one hath discovered, hath lifted the veil of glory, and uncovered the countenance of Beauty.'

"Within this Paradise, and from the heights if its loftiest chambers, the Maids of Heaven have cried out and shouted: 'Rejoice, ye dwellers of the realms above, for the fingers of Him Who is the Ancient of Days are ringing, in the name of the All-Glorious, the Most Great Bell, in the midmost heart of the heavens. The hands of bounty have borne round the cup of everlasting life. Approach, and quaff your fill. Drink with healthy relish, O ye that are the very incarnations of longing, ye who are the embodiments of vehement desire!'" [47]

Bahá'u'lláh, His family, and the small group of believers accompanying them stayed in Constantinople for only four months. The Persian Government continued from afar its persecution of the One it now clearly saw as the leader of the Bábí movement. Its ambassador in the court of the Sultan, the ruler of the Ottoman Empire, mounted a systematic campaign against Bahá'u'lláh. The environment in which the Sultan, his ministers and their associates lived was one of treachery, intrigue, and hypocrisy. Bahá'u'lláh refused to have anything to do with these unworthy people. His aloofness made it even easier for the Persian ambassador to fill the minds of the authorities with accusations and lies. His ceaseless efforts were effective and finally an order was issued exiling Bahá'u'lláh to the city of Adrianople, still farther from the Persian border.

Bahá'u'lláh's response to the order was an act of extraordinary courage. He immediately revealed a lengthy Tablet in which He addressed the Sultan himself, rebuked him and his ministers, and exposed their immaturity and incompetence. The Tablet was delivered to the Prime Minister in a sealed envelope. It is said that when he opened the letter and began to read it, he turned pale and remarked: "It is as if the King of Kings were issuing his behest to his humblest vassal king and regulating his conduct." [48]

The twelve-day journey from Constantinople to Adrianople was extremely difficult for Bahá'u'lláh and His family, who had now set out on their third exile. It was the month of December, and the weather was extremely cold. Most of the exiles did not have the necessary clothes to protect them from such harsh weather. Even to obtain water from springs on their way, they had to light a fire to thaw the ice.

Bahá'u'lláh entered Adrianople on 12 December 1863 and stayed in that city for a total of four and a half years. This period again was one of painful crises and splendid victories. As the influence of Bahá'u'lláh grew, the fire of jealousy burned more fiercely in Mirza Yahya's heart. He became bolder and bolder in his opposition and tried his best to prevent the Bábís from accepting the Manifestation of God for this Day. The trouble he caused not only affected the community itself, but also gave the external enemies of the Faith ammunition which they used to launch further attacks against Bahá'u'lláh and His followers. Mirza Yahya's treachery seemed to have no bounds. He even decided to poison Bahá'u'lláh, and schemed and worked until he finally achieved his purpose. The effect of the poison on Bahá'u'lláh was grave, and although He recovered, He was left with a shaking hand until the end of His life.

Adrianople, of course, will not be remembered for the shameful acts of Mirza Yahya, but for the great victories that Bahá'u'lláh achieved in that city. It was from here that Bahá'u'lláh sent many of His Tablets addressed to the kings and rulers of the world and proclaimed His Faith far and wide.

This public proclamation was the third stage of a gradual process through which Bahá'u'lláh's Mission was made known to humanity. The first stage began in the dungeon of Siyah-Chal in Tihran when the Divine Spirit revealed itself to Bahá'u'lláh and announced to Him that He was the Bearer of God's Message for today. Although the birth of His Revelation remained unknown for a decade, like the dawn, it stirred sleeping souls, gradually awakening the receptive ones and preparing them to recognize Bahá'u'lláh. The second stage opened in the Garden of Ridvan, where He declared His Mission to certain of the believers gathered to bid Him farewell. Now a small number of favored souls were aware of His Station. The third stage was the universal proclamation of His Mission. It began in Constantinople, gained considerable momentum in Adrianople, and reached its greatest heights of power in 'Akka, the next and final place of His exile.

Mirza Yahya's open opposition to Bahá'u'lláh in Adrianople caused great turmoil among the believers, many of whom were just beginning to get a glimpse of Bahá'u'lláh's Station. This gave the enemies of the Cause, who had behind them the powers of two governments-the Persian and the Ottoman-the opportunity they needed to strike another blow at the newly born Faith of God. Suddenly one morning, the house of Bahá'u'lláh was surrounded by soldiers, and everyone was told to prepare for immediate departure. For some time, no one knew what their destiny would be. The greatest fear of most was to be separated from their Beloved, for there were rumors that Bahá'u'lláh and His family would be exiled to one place and that the others would be forced to disperse. Finally, it became clear that Bahá'u'lláh was to be banished to the prison-city of 'Akka and Mirza Yahya to the island of Cyprus. Most of the exiles, numbering about seventy, were sent to 'Akka including the two most vicious supporters of Mirza Yahya. Four of the companions of Bahá'u'lláh, on the other hand, were exiled with Mirza Yahya's group to Cyprus.

Bahá'u'lláh and His family left Adrianople on 12 August 1868, and after a difficult journey by land and sea, arrived in 'Akka on 31 August. The inhabitants of 'Akka were accustomed to the arrival of prisoners, for the city was used by the Ottomans as a place of banishment for criminals and agitators. This time, they were told that the new arrivals were enemies of the State, of God and His religion. The Sultan had ordered to keep them in strict confinement, and he and his ministers had expressed the hope that the harsh conditions of 'Akka would lead to their eventual extermination. The order of the Sultan had been read publicly in the mosque, and it was understood by all that these Persians had been condemned to perpetual imprisonment and that association with them was strictly forbidden.

After disembarking at 'Akka, the exiles were taken to the army barracks, a section of which was to be their prison. The first night, they were deprived of food and drink, and afterwards they were each assigned three loaves of low-quality bread a day. Soon everyone, except for two, fell sick and, shortly after, three of them died. The guards refused to bury the dead without being paid the necessary expenses. A small prayer rug used by Bahá'u'lláh was sold, and the sum was given to the guards. Later, it was learned that they had not kept their word and had buried the dead unwashed, unshrouded and without coffins. They had in fact been given twice the amount required for the burial.

Although the conditions of imprisonment gradually improved, the first years in 'Akka were a period of severe suffering for Bahá'u'lláh. What He had endured in the SiyahChal had been inflicted upon Him solely by the external enemies of the Faith. The turmoil in Adrianople was internal in character. The crisis of those first years in 'Akka, however, was the result of the workings of both the external and internal enemies of the Faith. He Himself has referred to this period in words such as the following:

"Know thou that upon Our arrival at this Spot, We chose to designate it as the 'Most Great Prison'. Though previously subjected in another land to chains and fetters, We yet refused to call it by that name. Say: Ponder thereon O ye endued with understanding!" [49]

In spite of the order of the Sultan that no one should associate with Bahá'u'lláh and His family, a number of believers in Persia made the long journey to 'Akka, often on foot, with the hope that they might be admitted into His presence. Upon arrival, these devoted souls, unable to approach Him, would stand at a distance facing His prison, content to catch even a glimpse of His figure through the bars of His window. A wave of His blessed Hand was sufficient reward for months of travel, and most would then tum homeward, thankful for the bounty they had received.

The most tragic event of this period was the sudden death of Bahá'u'lláh's son Mirza Mihdi, known as the Purest Branch. One evening, he was on the roof of the barracks, pacing back and forth in prayer and meditation, when he fell through a skylight onto a wooden crate on the floor below. His ribs were pierced, and, though a doctor was called in, there was nothing to be done. Within twenty-two hours, he was dead. Before bis passing, Bahá'u'lláh asked the Purest Branch what he wished. He replied: "I wish the people of Baha to be able to attain Your presence." "And so it shall be," Bahá'u'lláh, said; "God will grant your wish." [50]

Severe as Bahá'u'lláh's sufferings were in the Most Great Prison, it must be remembered that His banishment to 'Akka was the fulfillment of the prophecies of the past. It was in 'Akka that the Sun of Truth would shine for twenty-four years in its full splendor. It would be during this period that while visiting Mount Carmel in nearby Haifa, Bahá'u'lláh would point out to 'Abdu'l-Baha the place where the Shrine of the Báb would later be built. It would be His own resting place situated in the vicinity of 'Akka that would constitute the Holiest Spot on earth and the Qiblih of the people of Baha. It would be in the vicinity of the Holy Shrine of the Báb that the Seat of the Universal House of Justice would be established. The twin cities of Haifa and 'Akka would become the spiritual and administrative world center of the Baha'i Faith. He had already alluded in a Tablet to His banishment to 'Akka saying that: "Up Our arrival We were welcomed with banners of light, whereupon the Voice of the Spirit cried out saying: 'Soon will all that dwell on earth be enlisted under these banners.'" [51]

In 'Akka Bahá'u'lláh continued His universal proclamation. Here are some passages He addressed from Adrianople and 'Akka to the kings and rulers of the world:

To the Emperor of the French, Napoleon III.

"O King of Paris! Tell the priest to ring the bells no longer. By God, the True One! The Most Mighty Bell hath appeared in the form of Him Who is the Most Great Name..." [52]

To Nicolaevitch Alexander II, the Czar of Russia:

"Arise thou amongst men in the name of this all-compelling Cause, and summon, then, the nations unto God, the Exalted, the Great." [53]

To Queen Victoria of England:

"Lay aside they desire, and set then thine heart towards thy Lord, the Ancient of Days. We make mention of thee for the sake of God, and desire that thy name may be exalted through thy remembrance of God, the Creator of earth and heaven." [54]

To William I, King of Prussia:

"Take head lest pride debar thee from recognizing the Dayspring of divine Revelation, lest earthly desires shut thee out, as by a veil, from the Lord of the Throne above and of the earth below." [55]

To Francis-Joseph, the Austrian Emperor:

"Open thine eyes, that thou mayest behold this glorious Vision, and recognize Him Whom thou invokest in the daytime and in the night-season, and gaze on the Light that shineth above this luminous Horizon." [56]

To Sultan 'Abdu'l-'Aziz of the Ottoman Empire:

"Lay not aside the fear of God, and be thou of them that act uprightly. Gather around thee those ministers from whom thou canst perceive the fragrance of faith and of justice, and take thou counsel with them, and choose whatever is best in thy sight, and be of them that act generously." [57]

To Nasiri'd-Din Shah of Persia:

"We pray that, out of His bounty—Exalted be He—He may release, through this imprisonment, the necks of men from chains and fetters, and cause them to turn, with sincere faces, towards His Face, Who is the Mighty, the Bounteous. Ready is He to answer whosoever calleth upon Him, and nigh is He unto such as commune with Him" 58

To the Rulers of America and the Presidents of its Republics:

"Bind ye the broken with the hands of justice, and crush the oppressor who flourisheth with the rod of the commandments of your Lord, the Ordainer, the All-Wise" 59

To Pope Pius IX:

"The Word which the Son concealed is made manifest. It hath been sent down in the form of the human temple in this day. Blessed be the Lord Who is the Father! He, verily, is come unto the nations in His most great majesty." 60

To the entire body of monks of the Christian Church:

"O concourse of monks! Seclude not yourselves in churches and cloisters. Come forth by My leave, and occupy yourselves with that which will profit your souls and the souls of men." 61

Four months after the sudden death of the Purest Branch, Bahá'u'lláh and His companions had to be removed from the barracks to make way for some army troops. He and His family were, placed in several houses for brief periods of time and finally moved into the house known today as the House of 'Abbud. They remained under watch and were surrounded by a population that, influenced by the orders of the Sultan, was unfriendly and hostile towards them.

With time, however, the people of 'Akka came to recognize the innocence of this small band of exiles from Persia, and the conditions of their confinement were eased. Much of the change was due to 'Abdu'l-Baha, who was very much in contact with the inhabitants of the city and was able to demonstrate to them the true motives of the Baha'is and the spirit of His Father's Teachings. Eventually, Bahá'u'lláh could leave the city of 'Akka and visit nearby places. Having been confined so long in the walls of a desolate city, Bahá'u'lláh could now pass some time in the countryside and enjoy the beauty and greenery of nature He so loved.

The last years of Bahá'u'lláh's life were spent in the Mansion of Bahji, just outside of 'Akka. Built while He was imprisoned within the city walls, it was abandoned by the owner when an epidemic broke out in the area. 'Abdu'l-Baha was able to acquire it for His beloved Father, first renting it and later purchasing it outright.

By now the attitude of the people of not only 'Akka but also the nearby regions of Syria and Lebanon towards Bahá'u'lláh and His followers had completely changed. Though the orders of the Sultan were still in effect, and formally He was a prisoner under strict confinement, He was, in reality, as revered and respected as a king. Even the officials of the region would come to seek His advice and counsel. Thus is the power of Bahá'u'lláh's Revelation to transform the hearts of men.

During the years in 'Akka and Bahji, the Pen of Bahá'u'lláh revealed volumes and volumes of guidance that will enable humanity to build a glorious world civilization. The mightiest of the Works to flow from His Pen was the Kitáb-i-Aqdas, the Most Holy Book of His Dispensation, revealed in the House of 'Abbud around 1873. Shoghi Effendi, referring to Bahá'u'lláh's Writings in the Holy Land, has said:

"The writings of Bahá'u'lláh during this period, as we survey the vast field which they embrace, seem to fall into three distinct categories. The first comprises those writings which constitute the sequel to the proclamation of His Mission in Adrianople. The second includes the laws and ordinances of His Dispensation, which, for the most part, have been recorded in the Kitáb-i-Aqdas, His Most Holy Book. To the third must be assigned those Tablets which partly enunciate and partly reaffirm the fundamental tenets and principles underlying that Dispensation." [62]

The great expansion of the Faith of Bahá'u'lláh into the Western World did not begin during His own lifetime and would have to await the period of 'Abdu'I-Baha's Ministry. His Teachings, however, had been introduced to countries of the West, and a few were aware of the Prisoner of 'Akka Who had remarkable influence on those with whom He came into contact. In the spring of 1890, towards the end of Bahá'u'lláh's life, Edward Granville Browne, a well-known scholar from Cambridge, England, came to meet Him. The following passages are from his record of that historic interview:

" ...my conductor paused for a moment while I removed my shoes. Then, with a quick movement of the hand, he withdrew, and, as I passed, replaced the curtain and I found myself in a large apartment, along the upper end of which ran a low divan, while on the side opposite to the door were placed two or three chairs. Though I dimly suspected whither I was going and whom I was to behold (for no distinct intimation had been given to me), a second or two elapsed ere, with a throb of wonder and awe, I became definitely conscious that the room was not untenanted. In the corner where the divan met the wall sat a wonderous and venerable figure, crowned with a felt head-dress of the kind called taj by dervishes (but of unusual height and make), round the base of which was wound a small white turban. The face of him on whom I gazed I can never forget, though I cannot describe it. Those piercing eyes seemed to read one's very soul; power and authority sat on that ample brow; while the deep lines on the forehead and face implied an age which the jet black hair and beard flowing down in indistinguishable luxuriance almost to the waist seemed to belie. No need to ask in whose presence I stood, as I bowed myself before one who is the object of a devotion and love which kings might envy and emperors sigh for in vain!

"A mild dignified voice bade me be seated, and then continued:—'Praise be to God that thou hast attained!... Thou hast come to see a prisoner and an exile...We desire but the good of the world and the happiness of the nations; yet they deem us a stirrer up of strife and sedition worthy of bondage and banishment...That all nations should become one in faith and all men as brothers; that the bonds of affection and unity between the sons of men should be strengthened; that diversity of religion should cease, and differences of race be annulled—what harm is there in this?... Yet so it shall be; these fruitless strifes, these ruinous wars shall pass away, and the 'Most Great Peace' shall come... Do not you in Europe need this also? Is not this that which Christ foretold?... Yet do we see your kings and rulers lavishing their treasures more freely on means for the destruction of the human race than on that which would conduce to the happiness of mankind... These strifes and this bloodshed and discord must cease, and all men be as one kindred and one family... Let not a man glory in this, that he loves his country; let him rather glory in this, that he loves his kind...'" 63

The Kitáb-i-Aqdas (which means "the Most Holy Book," or "the Book of Laws") is not a large book; it consists of only 190 paragraphs. In it, however, are contained the basic laws and ordinances of the future world civilization. Shoghi Effendi has referred to it as the Mother Book of Bahá'u'lláh's dispensation and the Charter of His New World Order. Here are the first five paragraphs of the Kitáb-i-Aqdas:

"The first duty prescribed by God for His servants is the recognition of Him Who is the Dayspring of His Revelation and the Fountain of His Laws, Who representeth the Godhead in both the Kingdom of His Cause and the world of creation. Whoso achieveth this duty hath attained unto all good; and whoso is deprived thereof hath gone astray, though he be the author of every righteous deed. It behooveth everyone who reacheth this most sublime station, this summit of transcendent glory, to observe every ordinance of Him Who is the Desire of the world. These twin duties are inseparable. Neither is acceptable without the other. Thus hath it been decreed by Him Who is the Source of Divine inspiration.

"They whom God hath endued with insight will readily recognize that the precepts laid down by God constitute the highest means for the maintenance of order in the world and the security of its peoples. He that turneth away from them is accounted among the abject and foolish. We, verily, have commanded you to refuse the dictates of your evil passions and corrupt desires, and not to transgress the bounds which the Pen of the Most High hath fixed, for these are the breath of life unto all created things. The seas of Divine wisdom and Divine utterance have risen under the breath of the breeze of the All-Merciful. Hasten to drink your fill, O men of understanding! They that have violated the Covenant of God by breaking His commandments, and have turned back on their heels, these have erred grievously in the sight of God, the All-Possessing, the Most High.

"O ye peoples of the world! Know assuredly that My commandments are the lamps of My loving providence among My servants, and the keys of My mercy for My creatures. Thus hath it been sent down from the heaven of the Will of your Lord, the Lord of Revelation. Were any man to taste the sweetness of the words which the lips of the All-Merciful have willed to utter, he would, though the treasures of the earth be in his possession, renounce them one and all, that he might vindicate the truth of even one of His commandments, shining above the Dayspring of His bountiful care and loving-kindness.

"Say: From My laws the sweet-smelling savor of My garment can be smelled, and by their aid the standards of Victory will be planted upon the highest peaks. The Tongue of My power hath, from the heaven of My omnipotent glory, addressed to My creation these words" 'Observe My commandments, for the love of My beauty.' Happy is the lover that hath inhaled the divine fragrance of his Best-Beloved from these words, laden with the perfume of a grace which no tongue can describe. By My life! He who hath drunk the choice wine of fairness from the hands of My bountiful favor will circle around My commandments that shine above the dayspring of My creation.

"Think not that We have revealed unto you a mere code of laws. Nay, rather, We have unsealed the choice Wine with the fingers of might and power. To this beareth witness that which the Pen of Revelation hath revealed. Meditate upon this, O men of insight!"[64]

Bahá'u'lláh's successive banishments, although apparently undertaken at the orders of worldly powers, were directed by the Hand of Almighty God Himself. The spiritual forces released as the Manifestation of God moved from place to place, finally arriving in the Holy Land where the spiritual and administrative center of His Faith was to be established, are incalculable!

During the years that a Manifestation of God walks among men, His extraordinary powers are diffused throughout the world, causing a profound change in the reality of all created things. In this Glorious Day, Bahá'u'lláh revealed the Word of God to humanity for almost forty years, endowing the world of being with limitless potentialities, the unfoldment of which will give rise to a civilization of unimaginable beauty. These forty years of continuous Divine Revelation came to an end on 29 May 1892.

Nine months before His ascension, Bahá'u'lláh had expressed His desire to depart from this world. From that time on, it became increasingly clear from the tone of the remarks He made, that the close of His life on this earthly plane was approaching. On the night of 8 May 1892, He contracted a slight fever. The fever grew the following day, but then seemed to go away. He continued to allow certain of the friends and pilgrims to meet with Him, but it soon became evident that He was not well. His fever returned, this time stronger than before, and His condition slowly grew worse. At the hour of dawn on 29 May 1892, in the 75th year of His life, His spirit ascended from this world.

Six days before He passed away, He called to His presence all the believers assembled in the Mansion of Bahji, for what was to be their last meeting with Him. As He lay in bed supported by one of His sons, He addressed them. "I am well pleased with you all" He said. "Ye have rendered many services and been very assiduous in your labors. Ye have come here every morning and every evening. May God assist you to remain united. May He aid you to exalt the Cause of the Lord of being."[65] Tears streamed from the eyes of those gathered around Him.

News of His passing was immediately communicated to the Sultan by telegram. The message began with the words "the Sun of Baha bas set" and went on to inform the Sultan of the plans to bury the sacred remains near the Mansion. A small room in a house just west of the Mansion was selected, and shortly after sunset on the very day of His ascension, His Body was laid to rest. The Qiblih of the people of Baha was now fixed at this Holy Spot. Nabil describes the agony of those days in these words: "Methinks, the spiritual commotion set up in the world of dust had caused all the worlds of God to tremble... My inner and outer tongue are powerless to portray the condition we were in.... In the midst of the prevailing confusion a multitude of the inhabitants of 'Akka and of the neighboring villages, that had thronged the fields surrounding the Mansion, could be seen weeping, beating upon their heads, and crying aloud their grief."[66]

For a full week, large numbers of mourners. rich and poor alike, came to express their grief to Bahá'u'lláh's family. Prominent people from all segments of society, including Muslims, Christians and Jews, poets, clergy, and government officials, joined in sorrowing over His loss and in praising His virtues and greatness. Many of them even paid written tributes to Him. Similar tributes were received from cities throughout the region, all of which were Submitted to 'Abdu'l-Baha, who now represented the Cause of Bahá'u'lláh. However, these expressions of sorrow were, in the words of the Guardian, "but a drop when compared with the ocean of grief and the innumerable evidences of unbounded devotion which, at the hour of the setting of the Sun of Truth, poured forth from the hearts of the countless thousands who had espoused His Cause, and were determined to carry aloft its banner in Persia, India, Russia, 'Iraq, Turkey, Palestine, Egypt and Syria."[67]

After Bahá'u'lláh's passing, Nabil was chosen by Abdu'l-Baha to select those passages that make up the text of the Tablet of Visitation which follows. This Tablet is recited in the Shrines of Bahá'u'lláh and the Báb. It is also frequently used in commemorating Their anniversaries. The Ascension of Bahá'u'lláh is commemorated in the early hours of 29 May.

"The praise which hath dawned from Thy most august Self, and the glory which hath shone forth from Thy most effulgent Beauty, rest upon Thee, O Thou Who art the Manifestation of Grandeur, and the King of Eternity, and the Lord of all who are in heaven and on earth! I testify that through Thee the sovereignty of God and His dominion, and the majesty of God and His grandeur, were revealed, and the Daystars of ancient splendor have shed their radiance in the heaven of Thine irrevocable decree, and the Beauty of the Unseen hath shone forth above the horizon of creation. I testify, moreover, that with but a movement of Thy Pen Thine injunction 'Be Thou' hath been enforced, and God's hidden Secret hath been divulged, and all created things have been called into being, and all the Revelations have been sent down.

"I bear witness, moreover, that through Thy beauty the beauty of the Adored One hath been unveiled, and through Thy face the face of the Desired One hath shone forth, and that through a word from Thee Thou hast decided between all created things, causing them who are devoted to Thee to ascend unto the summit of glory, and the infidels to fall into the lowest abyss.

I bear witness that he who hath known Thee hath known God, and he who hath attained unto Thy presence hath attained unto the presence of God. Great, therefore, is the blessedness of him who hath believed in Thee, and in Thy signs, and hath humbled himself before Thy sovereignty, and hath been honored with meeting Thee, and hath attained the good pleasure of Thy will, and circled around Thee, and stood before Thy throne. Woe betide him that hath transgressed against Thee, and hath denied Thee, and repudiated Thy signs, and gainsaid Thy sovereignty, and risen up against Thee, and waxed proud before Thy face, and hath disputed Thy testimonies, and fled from Thy rule and Thy dominion, and been numbered with the infidels whose names have been inscribed by the fingers of Thy behest upon Thy holy Tablets.

Waft, then, unto me, O my God and my Beloved, from the right hand of Thy mercy and Thy loving-kindness, the holy breaths of Thy favors, that they may draw me away from myself and from the world unto the courts of Thy nearness and Thy presence. Potent art Thou to do what pleaseth Thee. Thou, truly, hast been supreme over all things.

The remembrance of God and His praise, and the glory of God and His splendor, rest upon Thee, O Thou Who art His Beauty! I bear witness that the eye of creation hath never gazed upon one wronged like Thee. Thou wast immersed all the days of Thy life beneath an ocean of tribulations. At one time Thou wast in chains and fetters; at another Thou wast threatened by the sword of Thine enemies. Yet, despite all this, Thou didst enjoin upon all men to observe what had been prescribed unto Thee by Him Who is the All-Knowing, the All-Wise.

May my spirit be a sacrifice to the wrongs Thou didst suffer, and my soul be a ransom for the adversities Thou didst sustain. I beseech God, by Thee and by them whose faces have been illumined with the splendors of the light of Thy countenance, and who, for love of Thee, have observed all whereunto they were bidden, to remove the veils that have come in between Thee and Thy creatures, and to supply me with the good of this world and the world to come. Thou art, in truth, the Almighty, the Most Exalted, the All-Glorious, the Ever-Forgiving, the Most Compassionate.

Bless Thou, O Lord my God, the Divine Lote-Tree and its leaves, and its boughs, and its branches, and its stems, and its offshoots, as long as Thy most excellent titles will endure and Thy most august attributes will last. Protect it, then, from the mischief of the aggressor and the hosts of tyranny. Thou art, in truth, the Almighty, the Most Powerful. Bless Thou, also, O Lord my God, Thy servants and Thy handmaidens who have attained unto Thee. Thou, truly, art the All-Bountiful, Whose grace is infinite. No God is there save Thee, the Ever-Forgiving, the Most Generous." [68]

THE LIFE OF 'ABDU'L-BAHÁ

'ABDU'L-BAHÁ, THE PERFECT EXEMPLAR
On the evening of 22 May 1844, a significant moment in human history occurred. In the city of Shiraz, Iran, the Báb declared the beginning of a new religious cycle for the world.

At midnight, on that same evening, a Báby was born in Tehran. Bahá'u'lláh, in honour of His own father, named His newborn son, 'Abbás. But, in time, 'Abbás chose to call Himself 'Abdu'l-Bahá, the "Servant of Bahá", and, through His life of service to humanity, became known as the living embodiment and exemplar of Bahá'u'lláh's teachings.

Childhood

'Abdu'l-Bahá enjoyed a privileged childhood until fierce persecutions broke out against the Báb's followers—of whom Bahá'u'lláh was the most prominent. Bahá'u'lláh's incarceration for being a Bábí marked a turning point for His family. Seeing Bahá'u'lláh in prison—His hair and beard unkempt, His neck swollen from the heavy steel collar, His body bent by chains—made an indelible impression on the mind of His eight year-old son.

In December 1852, Bahá'u'lláh was released from prison after four months. Almost immediately, He was banished from Iran with His family. They were never to see their native land again. On the trek to Baghdad, 'Abdu'l-Bahá suffered frostbite and grieved over the separation from his Báby brother, Mihdí, who was not well enough to make the gruelling journey.

Soon after their arrival in Baghdad, another painful separation followed when Bahá'u'lláh retreated into the mountains of Kurdistan for a period of two years. With His beloved Father away, 'Abdu'l-Bahá occupied His time reading and meditating upon the Writings of the Báb.

Service to Bahá'u'lláh

When Bahá'u'lláh finally returned, the 12 year-old boy was overwhelmed with joy. Despite His tender age, 'Abdu'l-Bahá had already intuitively recognized the station of His Father. In the years that immediately followed, 'Abdu'l-Bahá became Bahá'u'lláh's representative and His secretary.

He shielded His Father from unnecessary intrusions and the malice of those who wished Him ill and became revered in circles beyond His Father's followers, conversing with the wise and learned on themes and topics that occupied their minds. One commentary He wrote while still in His teens demonstrated His already profound knowledge and understanding, and a striking mastery of language. Throughout their exiles, 'Abdu'l-Bahá also assumed the burden of various negotiations with civil authorities.

During Bahá'u'lláh's final banishment to 'Akká, 'Abdu'l-Bahá continued to protect His Father, took care of His followers, tended to the sick and the poor in the city, and held His ground on matters of justice with callous jailers, brutal guards and hostile officials. 'Abdu'l-Bahá's generosity of spirit, selfless service and adherence to principle endeared Him to those who came to know Him and, in time, won over even the most hard-hearted of enemies.

The Centre of the Covenant

In His Most Holy Book, Bahá'u'lláh established a covenant with His followers, enjoining them to turn, after His passing, to 'Abdu'l-Bahá, Who He describes as "Him Whom God hath purposed, Who hath branched from this Ancient Root." 'Abdu'l-Bahá's authority as the "Centre of the Covenant" was also established in other texts, including Bahá'u'lláh's Will and Testament.

From the time of Bahá'u'lláh's passing, 'Abdu'l-Bahá oversaw the spread of His Father's Faith to new territories, including North America and Europe. He received a steady flow of pilgrims from both the East and the West, carried out an extensive correspondence with Bahá'ís and inquirers in all parts of the world, and lived an exemplary life of service to the people of 'Akká.

Envious of 'Abdu'l-Bahá's influence, His younger half-brother—Mirza Muhammad 'Alí—tried to undermine and usurp 'Abdu'l-Bahá's authority. Efforts to stir up further suspicion against 'Abdu'l-Bahá in the minds of the already hostile authorities resulted in restrictions that had gradually been relaxed over the years being re-imposed. Although these attacks caused great pain to Him and His loyal followers, they failed to cause lasting damage to the unity of the community or the spread of the Bahá'í Faith.

Travel to the West

As early as 1907, 'Abdu'l-Bahá had begun moving His family to Haifa, across the bay from 'Akká, where He had built a house at the foot of Mount Carmel. In 1908, turmoil in the Ottoman capital culminated in the Young Turk Revolution. The Sultan released all of the empire's religious and political prisoners and, after decades of imprisonment and exile, 'Abdu'l-Bahá was free.

Despite tremendous challenges, work on a tomb for the Báb had proceeded, midway up the mountain, in a spot designated by Bahá'u'lláh Himself. In March 1909, 'Abdu'l-Bahá was able to place the Báb's remains in the Shrine He had constructed.

The following year, 'Abdu'l-Bahá departed Haifa for Egypt, where He stayed one year, spending His days meeting diplomats, intellectuals, religious leaders and journalists. In the late summer of 1911, He sailed for Europe, stopping at the French resort of Thonon-les-Bains before traveling to London.

On 10 September 1911, from the pulpit of the City Temple church in London, 'Abdu'l-Bahá gave a public address for the first time in His life. His subsequent month-long stay in England was filled with ceaseless activity, promoting Bahá'u'lláh's teachings and their application to many contemporary issues and problems, through public talks, meetings with the press and interviews with individuals. The days in London, and then Paris, set a pattern that He would follow throughout all of His travels.

In the spring of 1912, 'Abdu'l-Bahá journeyed to the United States and Canada for nine months. He travelled from coast to coast, addressing every kind of audience, meeting people of all ranks and stations. Adorned with flowing robes and a full white beard, this "Prophet of Peace" traveled to some 50 U.S. and Canadian cities, giving more than 140 public talks with a cumulative audience of about 93,000 people—from leaders of government and industry to servants, the poor and the homeless. He was acclaimed in hundreds of newspaper articles that trumpeted the arrival of the new religion's leader and His uplifting message for mankind. Headlines called Him the Prophet of Peace, the Apostle of Universal Peace and Brotherhood, the Persian Prophet, the Persian Sage and the new St. John the Baptist. He met prominent Americans like Alexander Graham Bell, Admiral Peary, Jane Addams, W.E.B. DuBois, Kahlil Gibran and Phoebe Hearst. In His addresses, Abdu'l-Baha warned of impending war, decried outmoded prejudices and hatreds, and outlined America's potential to lead the way toward a just and peaceful world. To achieve this destiny, He called for America to advance spiritually as well as materially. His Prayer for America expressed a galvanizing vision of America's spiritual destiny. At the end of the year, He returned to Britain and early in 1913, to France, from where He proceeded to Germany, Hungary and Austria, returning in May to Egypt, and on 5 December 1913, to the Holy Land.

'Abdu'l-Bahá's travels in the West contributed significantly to the spread of Bahá'u'lláh's teachings and the firm establishment of Bahá'í communities in Europe and North America. On both continents, He received a highly appreciative welcome from distinguished audiences concerned about the condition of modern society, devoted to such concerns as peace, women's rights, racial equality, social reform and moral development.

During His travels, 'Abdu'l-Bahá's message was the announcement that the long-promised age for the unification of humanity had come. He frequently spoke of the need to create the social conditions and the international political instruments necessary to establish peace. Less than two years later, His premonitions of a world-encircling conflict became a reality.

The Great War

When the First World War broke out, 'Abdu'l-Bahá's communication with the Bahá'ís abroad was almost completely cut off. He spent the war years ministering to the material and spiritual needs of the people around Him, personally organizing extensive agricultural operations, and averting a famine for the poor of all religions in Haifa and 'Akká. His service to the people of Palestine was honoured with a knighthood from the British Empire in April 1920.

During the war years, 'Abdu'l-Bahá produced one of the most important works of His ministry: fourteen letters, known collectively as the Tablets of the Divine Plan, addressed to the Bahá'ís of North America outlining the spiritual qualities and attitudes as well as the practical actions needed to spread the Bahá'í teachings throughout the world.

Final Years

In His old age, 'Abdu'l-Bahá remained remarkably vigorous. He was a loving father not only to the community of Bahá'ís in Haifa, but to a burgeoning international movement. His correspondence guided global efforts to establish an organizational framework for the community. His interaction with a stream of pilgrims to the Holy Land provided another instrument for instructing and encouraging believers from around the world.

When He passed away at the age of 77 on 28 November 1921, His funeral was attended by 10,000 mourners of numerous religious backgrounds. In spontaneous tributes to an admired personality, 'Abdu'l-Bahá was eulogized as One who led humanity to the "Way of Truth," as a "pillar of peace" and the embodiment of "glory and greatness."

'Abdu'l-Bahá's mortal remains were laid to rest in one of the chambers of the Shrine of the Báb on Mount Carmel.

THE LIFE AND WORK OF SHOGHI EFFENDI

Shoghi Effendi – The Guardian of the Bahá'í Faith
For 36 years—from 1921 until his passing in 1957—Shoghi Effendi immersed himself completely in the work he had been appointed to shoulder as Guardian of the Bahá'í Faith. His guiding hand directed the evolution and growth of the Bahá'í community throughout the world at a critical stage in its development.

Early Life

Related to both the Báb and Bahá'u'lláh, Shoghi Effendi was born in 'Akká while his Grandfather, 'Abdu'l-Bahá, was still a prisoner. From his earliest years, a staunchness of faith coupled with a deep devotion to his Grandfather motivated Shoghi Effendi's every action. He wished to master the English language so that he could serve as a secretary and translator for 'Abdu'l-Bahá, and so, in the spring of 1920, he left for Oxford University where he further developed his impressive command of English.

When 'Abdu'l-Bahá passed away in November 1921, Shoghi Effendi was devastated. In a state of profound grief, he learned that 'Abdu'l-Bahá in His Will and Testament had appointed him the Guardian of the Bahá'í Faith.

Despite his personal distress, Shoghi Effendi vigorously assumed his daunting responsibilities. He set out to execute the provisions of what he identified as three "charters" of the Bahá'í Faith: Bahá'u'lláh's Tablet of Carmel, establishing the mandate for the development of the Bahá'í World Centre in the Holy Land; The Will and Testament of

'Abdu'l-Bahá, outlining the framework for the evolution of the Bahá'í administration; and 'Abdu'l-Bahá's Tablets of the Divine Plan, providing the guidelines for the global expansion of the Bahá'í community.

With the passing of 'Abdu'l-Bahá, the Bahá'í Faith entered a new stage in its growth. What Shoghi Effendi described as its "apostolic era" or "heroic age" had passed, and its "formative age" had begun. His own position as Guardian involved a function and style of leadership quite different from that of 'Abdu'l-Bahá.

In 1937, Shoghi Effendi married Mary Maxwell from Montreal, Canada, who became known to Bahá'ís by the title Amatu'l-Bahá Ruhiyyih Khanum. Years later, in a message to the National Spiritual Assembly of the Bahá'ís of Canada, the Guardian described her as "my helpmate, my shield...and my tireless collaborator in the arduous tasks I shoulder."

Building the Bahá'í Administration

The development of Bahá'u'lláh's administrative order was a major focus of Shoghi Effendi's attention. As the Bahá'í institutions evolved, they would mobilize the community's human and material resources, providing the necessary instruments for the implementation of the Divine Plan. First, a structure of elected local and national Bahá'í institutions was required to administer the affairs of the growing community. Shoghi Effendi guided these nascent institutions to carry out a wide range of essential activities, such as promoting the teachings, publishing literature, and organizing community life—all the while learning how to practice the method of consultative decision making prescribed by Bahá'u'lláh.

In 1937, 16 years after the passing of 'Abdu'l-Bahá, the administrative capacity in a number of countries had developed sufficiently that Shoghi Effendi could begin implementing plans to diffuse the Bahá'í teachings further afield and establish communities throughout the entire planet, in fulfilment of the objectives laid out in the Tablets of the Divine Plan.

To spearhead and support this work, the Guardian began appointing the "Hands of the Cause of God", a corps of outstanding Bahá'ís on every continent, whom he later designated as the "Chief Stewards of Bahá'u'lláh's embryonic World Commonwealth". The function of this body of high-ranking believers was to lead initiatives in promoting the Bahá'í teachings, encourage learning, assist and educate the Assemblies in their duties, and provide moral leadership and encouragement. In 1951, Shoghi Effendi appointed the members of an International Bahá'í Council, which he described as the forerunner to the Universal House of Justice. In 1954, a global network of Auxiliary Board members to assist the Hands of the Cause was also formed.

Expansion of the Bahá'í Community

In order to realize the aims of 'Abdu'l-Bahá's Divine Plan—to establish the Bahá'í Faith in every land—the Guardian initially encouraged and assisted what was then a relatively small band of Bahá'ís to spread out across the planet. A few arose immediately. Foremost among them was an American journalist, Martha Root, who traversed the globe at least four times and shared the Bahá'í message with countless souls, among them Queen Marie of Romania—the first royal personage to embrace the teachings. Shoghi Effendi maintained regular correspondence with Martha Root and the numerous other intrepid individuals who left their homes to spread the Faith.

As the number of Bahá'ís—and their capacity to act—increased, Shoghi Effendi systematically set about putting 'Abdu'l-Bahá's plan (as set out in the Tablets of the Divine Plan) into effect, giving a series of specific plans to a number of national Bahá'í communities to spread the Faith further afield. By 1953, the Bahá'ís were able to embark upon what he described as a "fate-laden, soul-stirring, decade-long, world-embracing Spiritual Crusade". Through this campaign, the Bahá'ís throughout the world achieved astonishing results. When

'Abdu'l-Bahá had passed away, some 35 countries were already opened to the Bahá'í Faith with a few having rudimentary organization at the national level. By the time of Shoghi Effendi's passing in 1957, Bahá'ís resided in 219 new sovereign states, dependencies and major islands. By 1963, there were 56 nationally elected governing councils—known as National Spiritual Assemblies—as well as more than 4,500 Local Spiritual Assemblies, and Bahá'ís in more than 15,000 localities. Today the worldwide Bahá'í community has more than 5 million Bahá'ís residing in over 100,000 localities; Around 2,100 indigenous tribes, races, and ethnic groups represented; 188 National Spiritual Assemblies and 300 training institutes established.

The Bahá'í World Centre

During his ministry, Shoghi Effendi began to construct in the Holy Land the heart and nerve-centre of a world-embracing Faith, overcoming what often seemed to be insurmountable material obstacles.

Among the many tasks he shouldered in this regard, one was particularly weighty—to safeguard the Shrine of Bahá'u'lláh and the buildings and land adjoining it. Securing the entirety of the property, and beautifying its environs, was a task that occupied him until the end of his life.

In Haifa, he oversaw the construction of the superstructure for the Shrine of the Báb on Mount Carmel, which with its golden dome became known as the "Queen of Carmel". He also laid out magnificent gardens around both Shrines and acquired, restored and beautified many other sites associated with Bahá'í history, including the surroundings of the resting places of the sister, brother, mother, and wife of 'Abdu'l-Bahá.

To establish facilities for the world administrative centre of the Faith on Mount Carmel, Shoghi Effendi mapped out an "arc" on the mountainside, around which buildings housing the international institutions of the Bahá'í Faith would be situated. The first of these, the International Archives Building, was completed shortly before his passing.

Crises and Victories

Throughout Shoghi Effendi's ministry, he guided the Bahá'í community through numerous challenges: the German Bahá'ís were persecuted under Nazi rule; a number of Bahá'ís were arrested and interrogated in Turkey; the highly-developed community in 'Ishqábád—following sustained persecution by the Soviet authorities in the 1920s and 1930s—was dispersed; further opposition to the Faith broke out in Iran; the house of Bahá'u'lláh in Baghdad was seized and could not be regained.

With characteristic calm and perception, Shoghi Effendi saw the potential for triumph in every apparent crisis facing the Bahá'ís. For example, in Egypt the courts delivered a series of judgments which, while on the surface appeared to be adverse, were hailed by Shoghi Effendi as recognition of the independent nature of the Bahá'í Faith. While assisting the community to take action in national courts and on the international stage to defend their basic human rights, he also taught them to see difficulties as opportunities to carry forward the work of the Faith.

The Passing of Shoghi Effendi

Despite carrying the enormous burden of duties and responsibilities, the Guardian devoted whatever time he could spare to greeting pilgrims visiting the Holy Land from both East and West. He met with them, encouraged and advised them, and shared news of the progress of the community worldwide.

In November 1957—while he was visiting London for the purpose of purchasing furniture and ornaments for the buildings and gardens of the Bahá'í World Centre—Shoghi Effendi passed away suddenly at the age of 60. The Bahá'ís of the world were left in a state of profound grief. His final resting place is in the New Southgate Cemetery in north

London. Today, it is a place of prayer and reflection for visitors from all over the world.

THE STORIES OF "THE Life of the Báb and Bahá'u'lláh" were taken mostly but not all from "The Twin Manifestations Ruhi Institute Book 4.

If you would like to explore and expand more on the stories and histories of the Figures of the Baha'i Faith, the references that follow are a wonderful resource as are the friends for questions and meaningful dialogue. You can also visit the worldwide Baha'i community website at bahai dot org or the US website at Bahai dot us.

With Loving Regards,

Jeanie Halstead

REFERENCES FOR THE LIFE OF THE BÁB

1. *The Dawn-Breakers: Nabil's Narrative of the Early Days of the Baha'i Revelation* (Wilmette: Baha'i Publishing Trust, 1974), pp 75-76

2. Shoghi Effendi, *God Passes By* (Wilmette: Baha'i Publishing Trust, 1995), p xiv.

3. *The Dawn-Breakers*, p. 57.

4. Ibid., p. 63.

5. Ibid., p. 65.

6. *The Promulgation of Universal Peace: Talks Delivered by 'Abdu'l-Baha during His Visit to the United States and Canada in 1912* (Wilmette Publishing Trust, 1995), p. 138.

7. *The Dawn-Breakers*, pp. 85-86

8. Ibid., pp. 92-94

9. Ibid., pp. 142-43

10. Ibid., p. 146

11. *The Promulgation of Universal Peace*, p. 138.

12. *The Dawn-Breakers*, pp. 148-50.

13. Ibid., p. 198.

14. Ibid., p. 212.

15. Ibid., p. 213.

16. Ibid., p. 249.

17. Ibid., pp. 315-16.

18. *The Dawn-Breakers*, p. 507.

19. Ibid., p. 307-08.

20. Ibid., p. 508.
21. Ibid., p. 509.
22. Ibid., p. 512.
23. Ibid., p. 513.
24. Ibid., p. 514

REFERENCES FOR THE LIFE of BAHÁ'U'LLÁH

1. The Promulgation of Universal Peace: Talks Delivered by 'Abdu'l-Baha During His Visit to the United States and Canada in 1912 (Wilmette: Baha'i Publishing Trust, 1995), p.25.

2. From an unpublished translation of Bahá'u'lláh's tablet to Ra'is.

3. Ibid.

4. The Dawn-Breakers: Nabil's Narrative of the Early Days of the Baha'i Revelation (Wilmette: Baha'i Publishing Trust, 1974), p. 119.

5. The Dawn-Breakers, pp. 119-20.

6. Bahá'u'lláh, Epistle to the Son of the Wolf (Wilmette: Baha'i Publishing Trust, 1995), p.11.

7. 'Abdu'l-Baha on Divine Philosophy (Boston: tudor Press, 1918), p.49.

8. The Dawn-Breakers, p. 96.

9. Ibid., p. 104.

10. Ibid., pp. 104-05.

11. Ibid., pp. 105-06.

12. Ibid., p. 106.

13. Ibid., p. 107.

14. Ibid., p. 107.

15. Ibid., p. 107-08.

16. Selections from the Writings of the Báb (Haifa: Baha'i World

Centre, 1982), pp. 82-83.

17. Ibid., 98.

18. Ibid., 149.

19. The Dawn-Breakers, p. 113.

20. Ibid., p. 116.

21. Gleanings from the Writings of Bahá'u'lláh (Wilmette: Baha'i Publishing Trust, 1994), CXXIX, pp. 279-80.

22. The Promulgation of Universal Peace, pp. 141-42.

23. From a letter dated 29 August 1852 written by Captain Von Goumoens, cited in Shoghi Effendi, God Passes By (Wilmette: Baha'i Publishing Trust, 1995), pp. 65-66.

24. The Dawn-Breakers, pp. 607-08.

25. Tablets of Bahá'u'lláh Revealed after the Kitab-i-Aqdas (Wilmette: Baha'i Publishing Trust, 1994), p. 40.

26. Ibid., p. 96.

27. The Dawn-Breakers, p. 632.

28. Epistle to the Son of the Wolf, pp. 20-21.

29. The Dawn-Breakers, p. 631-33.

30. Epistle to the Son of the Wolf, p. 21.

31. Ibid., p. 22.

32. God Passes By, pp. 101-02.

33. Gleanings from the Writings of Bahá'u'lláh, XXIX, p. 72.

34. From a letter dated 24 June 1936 written on behalf of Shoghi Effendi to an individual believer, cited in the compilation, Crisis and Victory (London: Baha'i Publishing Trust, 1988), p. 15.

35. Balyuzi, H. M., Bahá'u'lláh: The King of Glory (Oxford: George Ronald, 1991), p. 104.

36. Bahá'u'lláh, cited in God Passes By, p. 109.

37. Bahá'u'lláh, The Kitab-i-Iqan (Wilmette: Baha'i Publishing Trust, 1993), p. 251.

38. God Passes By, p. 115.

39. Ibid., p. 137.

40. Epistle to the Son of the Wolf, p. 22.

41. The Kitab-i-Iqan, p. 3.

42. Bahá'u'lláh, The Hidden Words (Wilmette: Baha'i Publishing Trust, 1994), p. 3.

43. God Passes By, p. 144.

44. God Passes By, p. 147.

45. Bahá'u'lláh, The Kitab-i-Aqdas: The Most Holy Book (Wilmette: Baha'i Publishing Trust, 1993), p. 48.

46. God Passes By, p. 153.

47. Gleanings from the Writings of Bahá'u'lláh, XIV, pp. 27-32.

48. God Passes By, p. 160.

49. Bahá'u'lláh, cited in God Passes By, p. 185.

50. Bahá'u'lláh: The King of glory, pp. 311-13.

51. Bahá'u'lláh, cited in God Passes By, p. 184.

52. The Proclamation of Bahá'u'lláh (Haifa: Baha'i World Centre, 1967), p. 17.

53. Ibid., p.28.

54. Ibid., p. 33.

55. Ibid., p. 39.

56. Ibid., p. 43.

57. Ibid., p. 47.

58. Ibid., p. 60.

59. Ibid., p. 63.

60. Ibid., p. 84.

61. Ibid., p. 95.

62. God Passes By, pp. 205-06.

63. Bahá'u'lláh: The King of Glory, pp. 371-73.

64. The Kitab-i-Aqdas: The Most Holy Book, pp. 21-23.

65. God Passes By, p. 222.

66. Ibid., p. 222.

67. Ibid., p. 223.

68. Bahá'u'lláh, Baha'i Prayers: A Selection of Prayers Revealed by Bahá'u'lláh, The Báb, and 'Abdu'l-Baha (Wilmette: Publishing Trust, 1993), pp. 230-33.

www.ingramcontent.com/pod-product-compliance
Lightning Source LLC
Chambersburg PA
CBHW022157150726
47992CB00002B/834